# THE NATIONAL FORESTS OF AMERICA

*Weaver's Needle in the Superstition Mountains, Tonto National Forest, Arizona.*

# FORESTS OF AMERICA

By Michael Frome

Published by Country Beautiful Corporation
Waukesha, Wisconsin

COUNTRY BEAUTIFUL: *Publisher and Editorial Director:* Michael P. Dineen; *Executive Editor:* Robert L. Polley; *Senior Editors:* Kenneth L. Schmitz, James H. Robb; *Associate Editor:* Dorothy J. Hennessy; *Director of Sales:* John Dineen; *Executive Assistant:* Sharon G. Armao; *Circulation Manager:* Trudy Schnittka; *Fulfillment:* Marlene Yogerst; *Editorial Secretary:* Donna Johnson.

Maps by Blair Inc., Bailey's Crossroads, Virginia.

Country Beautiful Corporation is a wholly owned subsidiary of Flick-Reedy Corporation: President: Frank Flick; Vice President and General Manager: Michael P. Dineen; Treasurer and Secretary: August Caamano.

# CONTENTS

# INTRODUCTION

I am delighted to join with the Country Beautiful Foundation and G. P. Putnam's Sons in this, the story of our National Forests.

They are a uniquely American treasure—all 187 million acres of them—supplying the people of the nation with both natural resources and spiritual values that are without price.

I have traveled their paths, on foot, on horseback, by canoe, ever since boyhood in Minnesota. But not until I first visited Washington, many years ago, did I find a phrase that summed up my feelings about them. I found it on the huge painting, "Westward the Course of Empire Takes its Way," on the stairs of the House Gallery in the Capitol, in the words of Captain William Clark who led the way to the western ocean in the early years of the Republic:

> The spirit grows with its allotted space; the
> mind is narrowed in a narrow sphere.

The National Forests are lands of space to spare. Some of the trails that Clark and Meriwether Lewis traveled are still as they saw them, preserved for all time in the National Wilderness System, to inspire succeeding generations of Americans much as they must have inspired the empire builders of the last century.

Certainly I have been deeply inspired in many visits to these wild areas. Nothing I have been able to do as Secretary of Agriculture has given me more pleasure than adding, by executive order, another two million acres to the Wilderness System, and then seeing this system made permanent with passage of the Wilderness Act of 1964.

Other portions of the National Forests serve the physical needs of this generation—providing the timber, preserving the watersheds, that a nation of 200 million requires. Through intensive conservation efforts they will continue to provide for generations of Americans yet unborn.

The National Forests are the physical embodiment of a dream extant from the earliest days of the Republic. A century ago Henry David Thoreau, that apostle of man's harmony with nature, wrote:

"The kings of England formerly had their forests to hold the king's game for sport and food, sometimes destroying villages to create or extend them.

"Why should not we, who have renounced the king's authority, have our national preserves, where no villages need be destroyed, in which the bear and the panther may still exist, and not be civilized off the face of the earth—our own forests, not to hold the king's game merely, but for inspiration and our own true creation?"

Thoreau was gone by the time the National Forests were established, but surely his ideas must have inspired those who followed him.

Foremost among these was Gifford Pinchot, founder of scientific forestry in the United States and first Chief of the Department of Agriculture's Forest Service. Of him, President Theodore Roosevelt wrote, "He was the foremost leader in the great struggle to coordinate all our governmental forces in the effort to secure the adoption of a rational and far-seeing policy for securing the conservation of all our natural resources. He was practically breaking new ground."

In the generations before Pinchot the nation was intent on self-exploitation, expansion and immediacy, without thought of providing for the future. A few lonely voices spoke out—William Bartram, the colonial naturalist; Emerson and Thoreau; George Catlin, the frontier artist; and George Perkins Marsh, who warned that civilizations down through history rise or fall on their respect—or lack of respect—for natural resources. Few listened. Millions of acres of land passed from public ownership into concentrations of large private holdings and in the process, vast fortunes were amassed. The forests were devastated by logging and by fires that followed logging. The grassy plains and prairies were reduced to desert by millions of livestock. Fragile alpine slopes, where rivers are born, were cleft by the hooves of sheep and by the picks and shovels of hardy, and sometimes foolhardy, mining men, thus destroying whole watersheds.

In 1871 the nation was shocked by the worst fire in U. S. history, at Peshtigo, Wisconsin, where 1,500 persons died and nearly 1.3 million acres went up in smoke.

*Right: In the early years of our nation, only a few courageous voices declared the need to preserve our forests.*

Four years later the American Forestry Association was founded and at once heeded a plea from Carl Schurz, the German-born Secretary of the Interior, to reverse the tide of public opinion that "looked with indifference on this wanton, barbarous, disgraceful vandalism; a spendthrift people recklessly wasting its heritage; a Government careless of its future."

Spurred by the interest of this young association, Congress in 1876 authorized a special agent in the Department of Agriculture to deal exclusively with forest problems. Ten years later the Division of Forestry was established. Still, forest devastation and land fraud persisted. Some of the finest timberlands of the West, towering virgin redwoods, Douglas fir and white pine, were picked up for next-to-nothing by lumber companies that subverted the laws. Although the Timber and Stone Act provided that any citizen desiring to settle on the land could purchase 160 acres at $2.50 an acre, if he would pledge not to pass the title to anyone but would use the timber and stone materials himself, it was all too simple for companies to move in dummy "entrymen" by the trainload. Swearing that the new land was for personal use, they proceeded to transfer title to a lumber company and collect their fees.

But in 1891 Congress acted on the recommendations of the American Forestry Association and others to set aside large timbered areas of the West, upsetting the previous pattern of disposing of the public domain, virtually giving it away to encourage settlement. Now President Harrison had the authority to make withdrawals and to establish Forest Reserves.

The first unit adjoined Yellowstone National Park, which had been withdrawn earlier, in 1872. In the new Yellowstone Timberland Reserve (later to become Shoshone and Teton National Forests), President Harrison established reserves totalling 13 million acres. His successor, Grover Cleveland, added 21 million acres. Then came Theodore Roosevelt. He is remembered for lasting achievements on many fronts, but conservationists consider his setting aside 132 million acres of Forest Reserves the most significant achievement of all.

Roosevelt was a singular figure—sportsman, rancher, scholar, explorer and a maverick politician who combined idealism with pragmatism in meeting the issues of his time. In Gifford Pinchot, who had studied at the National School of Forestry in France, he found a kindred spirit.

*Famous Glacier Peak seen from Image Lake in the Mount Baker National Forest, Washington.*

*The cold but awesome beauty of High Sierra Wilderness Area is seen at Beetle Bug Lake at the head of Long Canyon.*

Secretary of Agriculture James Wilson appointed Pinchot head of the Department's Division of Forestry in 1898, and the new forester promptly launched a crusade "to get forestry from the books into the woods" by offering practical assistance to farmers, lumbermen, and state and local governments.

His main interest, however, lay in management of the Forest Reserves. While the Department of Agriculture had virtually all the foresters in Government service and responsibility for activity relating to crops, the reserves were administered by the General Land Office of the Department of the Interior. Pinchot was convinced the reserves should be shifted to Agriculture and received powerful support from President Roosevelt and the American Forestry Association. Congress approved the transfer on February 1, 1905. The Bureau of Forestry became the Forest Service and two years later the reserves were renamed as National Forests.

Gifford Pinchot gave long and distinguished service to his profession and to the nation. He defined the word conservation in its broadest sense. It came to him as a revelation while on a horseback trip through Rock Creek Park in Washington, D.C.

"Suddenly the idea flashed through my mind," he wrote later, "that there was a unity in this complication —that the relation of one resource to another was not the end of the story. Here were no longer a lot of different, independent and often antagonistic questions, each on its own little island, as we have been in the habit of thinking. In place of them, here was one single question with many parts. Seen in this new light, all these separate questions fitted into and made up the one great central problem of the use of the earth for the good of man."

He saw clearly that productive forests, pure air, clean water, stable soils, abundant wildlife, natural beauty and the opportunity for man to live in harmony with the natural environment are not only essential, but are also mutually supporting objectives. This "ecological conscience"—an awareness of the balanced interrelationship of all living things in their native environment —still guides conservationists today.

11

*Dixie National Forest, Utah: This craggy, multi-hued amphitheatre is on fork of Lower Robinson Creek.*

*Table Top Plateau, Dixie National Forest: From the top of mesa to base of cliff measures 2,000 feet.*

*Dramatic overhang in Echo Amphitheatre of
New Mexico's Carson National Forest.*

*Brilliant red of the dogwood enlivens the
fall in Jefferson National Forest.*

*Majestic view of the south end of Oak Creek Canyon in the Coconino National Forest, Arizona.*

*Mt. St. Helens, Pinchot National Forest, Washington, viewed across many miles of tall timber.*

Pinchot was far more than a technician. He was by instinct a social worker and social reformer. At one stage of his youth he had been undecided about following medicine or the ministry. Later he worked in settlement houses in the New York ghetto. He saw conservation as the cause of the many, rather than of the privileged few; he saw the National Forests as the peoples' forests.

Pinchot's autobiography, *Breaking New Ground,* was aptly named, for he was a prophet who inspired others to break new ground, to open the way from forest management into other fields. Thus from the National Forests have come Aldo Leopold, the leader in modern wildlife management; Robert Marshall, who made vital contributions to the concept of wilderness protection; and Benton MacKaye, a giant in regional planning and environmental design.

Leopold led the way in game conservation during the 1920's in the National Forests of the Southwest. His ecological ideas, set forth later in books and articles while he was a professor at the University of Wisconsin, still guide wildlife managers. He taught the interdependence of all living things, from arrow-weed thickets and cottonwoods to raccoons, skunks, avocets, heron, deer—and wolves and mountain lions. "The last word in ignorance," he wrote, "is the man who says of a plant or animal, 'what good is it?' If the land mechanism as a whole is good, then every part of it is good, whether we understand it or not."

Marshall, Chief of Recreation of the Forest Service during the 1930's, was the first to define wilderness as a practical, useful national resource. His philosophy and forcefulness contributed to regulations under which more than 14 million acres of National Forest have been protected as wilderness since 1939. He was one of the founders of the Wilderness Society, and one of the fathers of the historic Wilderness Act of 1964.

MacKaye, now almost 90, continues to point with pride to his early years as one of Gifford Pinchot's "young men." From 1905 to 1918 his main activity in the Forest Service was reclaiming and improving the forests of America. But he also addressed himself to the problem of how to use the natural resources of the nation without defacing the landscape, polluting the atmosphere, or disrupting the complex association of plant and animal upon which life itself depends.

As early as 1921, MacKaye outlined his ideas for the Appalachian Trail from Main to Georgia, a magnificent project of regional planning, which he conceived as the backbone of a whole system linked together by feeder trails. As a regional planner, he was peer and intimate of creative men like Lewis Mumford, Stuart Chase and Clarence Stein; he and others built on the foundation of early conservationists to devise important measures of the 1930's, the Tennessee Valley Authority, rural electrification, rural resettlement, flood control, shelter belts, the Civilian Conservation Corps, and a series of regional planning studies.

Today, the Forest Service is USDA's largest agency. It administers 187 million acres in 41 states and Puerto Rico. The National Forests are many things to many people—timber, water and forage, scenic beauty, the recognition of wildlife as a cultural and ethical value as well as a resource for hunting enjoyment; the identification and protection of botanical, biological and geological features.

Our foresters and other specialists are also enlarging our knowledge of man's history. Some of the oldest shell mounds of the East and cliff dwellings of the West are contained within the National Forests. So are the trails of Henry Rowe Schoolcraft who searched for the headwaters of the Mississippi River, of Zebulon Pike and John Frémont in surveying the highest peaks of the Rocky Mountains, and of Lewis and Clark in their epochal exploration to the Pacific—and so too are the vestiges of miners, forty-niners and overland pioneers who followed in their pathways.

The Department of Agriculture's sister agency, the Department of Interior, administers some 27 million acres through its Park Service. This agency's primary purpose is to preserve choice, superlative examples of natural beauty and historic significance for observation, appreciation and study. Geological features, plant and animal life are protected. The National Parks and National Monuments are outdoor museums in which commercial operations and hunting are for the most part prohibited.

The National Forests and National Grasslands, covering seven times as much land as the National Parks, are dedicated to the principle of conservation through use, a variety of balanced, or multiple uses—protecting the watersheds of hundreds of cities, furnishing timber, rangeland for livestock, homeland for wildlife, sources of minerals, breathing space and roaming room for a growing nation.

In recent years both agencies, at the direction of Congress, are administering new National Recreation Areas. The agencies cooperate closely. The Forest Service has benefited from the long background of the Park Service in museum and interpretive work. The Park Service has been able to observe methods of wilderness management developed in the National Forests. If there is rivalry, it is because the men are proud of their separate organizations and loyal to them. But it is a healthy rivalry, spurring both services to do a better job, affording the public a standard of comparison between them. On numerous trips to areas where National Parks and National Forests adjoin, I find rangers working harmoniously to solve their common problems, and much too busy to weigh any philosophic differences. They are establishing joint

*The pronghorn, also called the American antelope, is found in Gallatin National Forest, Montana, and others.*

visitor centers, exchanging personnel at campfire lectures, coordinating the flow of visitors into campgrounds, conducting joint studies of wildlife migrations and habitat, and participating in a host of common programs that increase their effectiveness and service to the taxpayer.

The National Forests face staggering challenges if they are to meet the demands of the future. Skyrocketing U.S. population, higher incomes and more leisure time mean an estimated 300 per cent increased demand for recreation in the next 32 years. The same forces, by the year 2000, will double the demand for food and wood products and triple the demand for water, to name just three. And all of this increased demand—

for recreation and for natural resources—must be satisfied from a fixed amount of American land.

Although we live in an expanding economy, the amount of land available to each of us is, in effect, shrinking: In 1900, if one had divided the total amount of U.S. land evenly among the population, each American would have had 25 acres. By 1930, as a consequence of expanding population, he would have had 13; today only 9.7 acres.

By the year 2000, each American will be able to command only 6.4 acres to feed, clothe, and shelter him; to produce the industrial products and natural resources he needs; to find the recreation that is almost a necessity in an increasingly mechanized world.

The National Forests—187 million acres of them—will be a treasure almost beyond price for the nation of 300 million souls that the United States will become in another three decades. With continued wise use and extensive conservation efforts, they will serve three Americans for every two alive today.

But beyond that, the National Forests can play a key role in what John Fischer of *Harper's* Magazine called "a new national purpose . . . to resettle the deserted hinterland, to discover ways of moving people and jobs away from megalopolis before it becomes both uninhabitable and ungovernable."

The description is apt. Today, 70 per cent of the U.S. population lives on less than 2 per cent of the U.S. land area, mainly crowded into very large urban aggregations. In another 32 years, if present trends continue, another 80 million new Americans will join the 140 million already in megalopolis, exacerbating already intolerable problems of crowding, social disruption, pollution of the environment and overcrowding.

But this doesn't have to be.

It *is* possible to allow Americans more freedom of choice on where they live—in the city or country—and to provide the jobs, cultural and educational facilities, and community facilities that make rural and small town life as attractive as that in the large city.

Literally hundreds of these towns already exist, many of them dependent upon the National Forests for some or most of their livelihood. A number of examples come to mind, one of the best-known being Aspen, Colorado; once a booming silver town, then a ghost town, with only a handful of inhabitants, now once again booming, a ski resort city utilizing runs in White River National Forest. Just over a mountain range or two, the glittering new town of Vail, Colorado, is also rising near the slopes of White River, testimony that rural America is Growth Country, USA.

Further south, near Oxford, Mississippi, concepts pioneered on the National Forests—sustained timber yield and multiple use—were instrumental in establishing a new, multi-million dollar flakeboard plant that is giving that town's economy a shot in the arm. Utilizing

*A profusion of daisies adds charm and gaiety to an unspoiled wilderness area.*

*Ottawa National Forest provides good sport as well as relaxation. Here a fisherman paddles along Fisher Lake looking for bass.*

timber on nearly half a million acres planted some years ago to stabilize a severely eroded watershed, the plant will harvest some 130,000 cords of pulpwood a year, most of it from private owners in the area. Many government agencies cooperated in this project, many new jobs have resulted, and numerous woodlot owners now have a market for their produce.

Human lives—as well as natural resources—are being saved in the National Forests. Last year, in some 47 Forest Service-operated Job Corps Centers literally thousands of poor young men were given a second chance; an opportunity to learn good work habits, and skills needed to make a living. Many were given special remedial help in reading; some saw doctors or visited dentists for the first time in their lives.

While they learned, they also helped conserve resources, building hundreds of new picnic and camping facilities, conserving watersheds, and doing a thousand-and-one other jobs that need doing on the public lands.

These are a few examples of how the National Forests and forest-related industries are contributing to an America in which population—and the jobs and facilities to support it—is widely scattered over available space, rather than concentrated, as now, in a few teeming cities. If we are ever to solve many of the problems that confront us—poverty in the ghettos, impaction in the cities and depopulation of rural areas—we shall have to do a great deal more of it in the next few years. The National Forests will be key to this effort in many places.

If this book contributes in any small way to a better understanding of our National Forests, if it encourages more Americans to visit them, then our purpose will have been accomplished.

For they must be seen and experienced to be understood. Those who have tramped the slopes of the North Cascades as I have—passing through successive life zones in a single day, smelling the pine, holding a pebble polished by eons of time—will know of what I speak. Those who have seen sunrise over the Continental Divide, heard the wind above timberline, a voice like all the rivers in the world flowing over a thousand miles of granite and green, know the priceless heritage that is ours in the National Forests.

The National Forests must be experienced with all the senses to be appreciated, and they must be appreciated if we are to maintain and preserve them for millions of Americans who will follow us.

*Right: Fisherman on Icicle River in Wenatchee National Forest, Washington.*

# I | The Tree and the Forest

The Swiss have a special word, *Krummholz*. It means, literally, "crooked wood," but it refers to the dwarfed trees of gnarled shapes found in the Alpine mountains.

*Krummholz* reveals to the Swiss a lot about a tree and the setting in which it grows.

It tells them that here is a hardy species clinging tenaciously to life. It is a conifer, for a deciduous tree could not survive in such a harsh environment. The tree has withstood long icy winters and the flailing of many high winds, and has bent before the sculpture of these forces into a contorted shape. It grows extremely slowly in rocky, infertile soil, yet it will endure through a long life.

The earth thus unfolds itself to the viewer through the trees and forests that it produces. It speaks of rocks and their history, of weather, of soils, of water, and of all kinds of life forms, because trees never grow alone but are part of a life community.

Some plants and trees are ancient forms, others are still in the process of evolution. The oldest class of trees is the conifer, which grew abundantly over the earth in the Jurassic Age, 175 million years ago. In the Cretaceous period, roughly 95 million years ago, the angiosperm, the complex flowering plant, originated and spread out, displacing ferns and the ancient conifers. The climate of the succeeding Tertiary was equable and mild over much of the earth; many species of deciduous trees, those that shed their leaves periodically, had a continuous distribution from North America across Europe to temperate Asia. Then came the frigid glacial ages, driving out the deciduous species and opening the way for the conifers. Today's vast forests of pine, spruce, fir and hemlock grow largely where the climate is cold, dry and windy, and in moderate climates, like the coastal plains and piedmont and the Southwest, where the soil is poor and sandy. They can survive where moisture is concentrated in winter snow, while the broadleaf trees require some moisture throughout the year. Conifers and hardwoods tend to replace each other. Even now the coniferous forests are slowly retreating northward as the earth's climate is warming again. Moving in behind them are the deciduous trees, for they are better adapted to dominate the habitats which conifers once ruled as their own.

A tree, any tree, is a thing of beauty in its own right. The sturdy, stately sugar maple, for instance, may be seen in spring sending forth myriads of greenish-yellow clustered flowers, from which bees obtain pollen and nectar. In early summer, seeds mature and fall to the ground on papery wings. Later, in autumn, sugar residue in heart-shaped leaves produces the most striking orange-yellows and reds of the hardwood landscape. The quaking aspen is an almost universal friend of the traveler—this white-trunked, fluttering-leafed tree greets one wherever he goes, from Labrador and the southern shore of Hudson Bay northwest to the Arctic Circle in Alaska, south through the mountains into Lower California, then scattering eastward across the northern plains to New England and the southern Appalachians.

Notwithstanding the welcome attractiveness of the tree to the eye, however, it becomes more meaningful and expressive when viewed in its relation to the life community and the construction of natural history.

The forest is a community, or complex of communities, of interdependent plants and animals. The foundation common to all is soil, sunlight and water, plus influences of climate, weather, erosion and reproduction cycles. The food chain is the tie that binds all life forms together, and plants provide the basic food. Thus the making of a forest environment begins with simple plant forms. One can witness the early process of plant succession in an area where a glacier is retreating—the start of a new virgin forest—or where fire has left its mark. When the soil has acquired sufficient texture and nutrients, it develops green plants capable of manufacturing food by taking carbon dioxide from the air and water from the soil. If the soil is good, and the plants can produce proteins, fats, sugars, starches and vitamins, chances are good for the health and prosperity of the entire forest community.

An acre of healthy soil is densely populated with millions of insects and tiny animals, diligent architects and engineers, who sift air and water and when they die return valuable minerals to build the soil to support higher life forms, including the highest form of plant life, the tree.

*Right: "The Old Ranger," an ancient bristlecone pine in Patriarch Grove, shows the beauty of grotesqueness.*

*This stand of white pine was planted in North Carolina 80 years ago. The roadside shrubbery is Deutzia of the hydrangea family.*

Protection of the soil is paramount in the National Forests. Soil-binding plants provide the most dependable check on erosion known to man. As Gifford Pinchot wrote in 1907, the main objectives in establishing National Forests were to prevent their destruction by fire and reckless cutting, "to save the timber for the use of the people and to give out steady flows of water for use in the fertile valleys below." All of these missions point to one focus: protecting the living mantle of the earth.

National Forests comprise the largest integrated timber reservoir in the world, an important source of wood for the nation and of economic stability to many communities. But they are also life communities, environments of nature and man, where the value of the immediate timber yield must be balanced with the long-range values in protecting soil, water, wildlife and scenery, and in assuring that the harvested areas will grow more trees for future timber needs.

In this context, timber cutting is regarded by the well-rounded forester as a tool, rather than an end in itself. In some circumstances it is a highly desirable tool. Thinning the number of trees reduces competition in the forest; it enables those trees that remain to grow stronger and faster, and it stimulates the growth of new seedlings. It provides sunny openings and borders where grass, plants and herbs can serve as food for wildlife. Logging provides the beginning of road systems to help visitors enjoy the National Forests. Such roads are used by sportsmen to harvest game species each year, thereby helping to keep the wildlife population within the ecological carrying capacity of the land, enabling it to sustain each species adequately, and also by campers and picnickers. In other circumstances, however, there may be no cutting at all: on sites where timber quality is poor and uneconomical to harvest, particularly when weighed against natural values; along streamsides, cutting is tailored to protect the fisheries habitat. Sport fishing is a prime form of National Forest recreation. Salmon, which spawn in Western mountain waters, have a high commercial value. Soil erosion, sometimes a problem in high mountain watersheds, leads to heavy siltation of streams and lakes, but fish life can be maintained only if waterways are kept in a clean, healthy condition. Therefore, it is a must for forest management to protect the flow and quality of water.

*(Continued on page 27)*

*California's giant sequoias, or "bigtrees," are the biggest and among the oldest trees.*

*Fireweed provides splash of color against fog-enshrouded hill of Western hemlock in Washington's Olympic National Forest.*

*Inyo National Forest, California: Bristlecone pines in Patriarch Grove at 11,000 feet are among world's oldest living things.*

*Chippewa National Forest, Minnesota: The paper birch has widest natural range of American birches.*

*Fall color of deciduous tree contrasts with surrounding Eastern white pine in Superior National Forest.*

National Forests conduct 25,000 sales of timber each year to large and small operators. Receipts for this "stumpage," or standing timber, range as high as $140 million in a year. These funds are earned for the Federal treasury, with 25 per cent returned to the states for use by counties in which the Forests are located for county roads and school programs. This is a considerable contribution, although in this age benefits of the National Forests can be measured in broader terms. Forests enhance the quality of community life, affording open space at one's doorstep and a backyard as big as all outdoors. For communities hitherto dependent on timber, the scenic, wildlife and wilderness resources of the National Forests constitute an economic asset of unlimited potential. And for the nation, the roving room and educational resourses have values that defy economic calculation.

In the harsh habitat of the desert, all life forms struggle for their share of the scant food and water supplies. They must adjust to a hot, dry world—plenty of sunlight, but not much water. Rain falls rarely, then in torrents. Most animals avoid the heat and conserve water by moving about at night and lying low during the daylight. Some, like the kangaroo rat, have learned the secret of surviving without ever drinking water. Certain plants become dormant, seemingly lifeless, during dry periods, then suddenly sprout leaves when the moisture level rises. Others, the succulents, store water in their stems, roots or leaves. The cacti have adapted to life without leaves, in order to reduce transpiration, or "exhaling."

Following soaking rains, the gigantic, towering saguaro cactus, the largest tree in the American desert, draws in immense quantities of moisture. A saguaro that weighs from six to ten tons may absorb as much as a ton of water into its widespread root system. In excessive rainfalls, some greedy saguaros drink so much they split open at the seams.

The saguaro dwells in the Lower Sonoran life zone, one of the seven divisions of plant and animal life ranging from Mexico to the Arctic Circle. These are determined principally by climate and rainfall. What plants and trees grow where within the life zone is determined by temperature, light and wind, the slope, drainage and physical composition of the soil. Thus, except for one or two spots in California, the saguaro is limited to northwestern Mexico and southern Arizona, reaching its greatest concentration in the Tucson area. Outside of that city, at Sabino Canyon, in Coronado National Forest, saguaros stand in large groves like a forest of gnarled primitive pillars, grotesque in a sense, but overwhelming in beauty, too, when blooming with creamy white flowers of springtime.

*Supplying lumber for the nation's needs is one aspect of the multiple-use concept that guides the National Forest System.*

From Sabino Canyon, the Hitchcock Highway winds to the summit of Mount Lemmon, a climb of almost 6,000 feet, a vertical ascent through four of the seven life zones. The three not represented are Dry-tropical, characterized by less than six inches of rain, and the Hudsonian and Arctic-Alpine, by more than 30 inches.

At 2,300 feet, with only ten inches of rainfall, the landscape is semi-desert—mesquite, creosote bush, yucca, palo verde, ocotillo, cottonwood in the stream channels and 25 types of cactus, from tiny pincushions to the saguaro growing to 40 or 50 feet in height. At 5,000 feet, the Molino Basin lies in the Upper Sonoran zone, with pinyon, juniper and oak chaparral sustained by 16 to 20 inches of rainfall. At 8,000 feet, in the Transition zone, where the annual precipitation is almost 25 inches, the ponderosa pine grows on south and west exposures. This hardy tree requires little water. Tenaciously the seedling withstands drought, often surviving only on the dew of night. A year-old tree will sink its roots two feet deep in search of water. The ponderosa pine grows in every state west of the Great Plains, but the southern Arizona tree bears only slight resemblance to its more favored brothers of the resin-scented California Sierra forests, which grow over 200 feet tall and live 500 years. Nor does the Douglas fir struggling for the sunlight of the north and east exposures bear strong resemblance to its brothers of the Northwest rain forests. At 9,100 feet, Mount Lemmon lies in the Canadian zone with more vigorous stands of pine and Douglas fir, as well as white fir and quaking aspen. The annual precipitation is 30 inches and most of it comes in the form of snow. In fact, Mount Lemmon is a popular winter ski center, a Canadian island overlooking the vast southeastern Arizona desert.

High in the White Mountains above Owens Valley the landscape is bleak and severe. This region is one of the remotest in California. Here, in the Ancient Bristlecone Pine Forest, are the oldest known living things on earth. Some of the trees found at this location have been growing more than 4,000 years. Methuselah, the oldest, has been dated at 4,600 years, a thousand years older than the oldest redwood. They are not, however, stately giants like the redwoods, but gnarled and twisted into many shapes and forms, and only 25 to 30 feet in height. The bristlecone pines have survived the most adverse conditions on exposed ridges of shallow, rocky soil, with little rainfall, and high winds as an almost constant companion.

The Ancient Forest was set aside within Inyo National Forest in 1958 as a botanical area for scientific study and public enjoyment, after scientific research had discovered the amazing age of the trees. They grow at elevations above 9,000 feet, accessible by a road that starts at 4,000 feet and rises almost to 12,000, with views of the immense eastern escarpment of the High Sierras, including Tioga Pass, the jagged Minarets and Palisade glacier, the southernmost in the United States. Bristlecone pine also grows in scattered stands in high mountain areas of the Southwest, but this seems the appropriate setting for the masters of the tribe.

*Quaking aspen, the best known of the trembling trees, along the stream Rio Hondo in Carson National Forest.*

*Left: Large trees in Sequoia National Forest are (left to right) incense cedar, ponderosa pine and sugar pine.*

Limber pines appear at the lower levels of the Ancient Forest; however, there is no mistaking them for bristlecones. The limber is readily seen to be a younger tree. It can be differentiated from the bristlecone by the short tufts of needles at the end of branchlets; while the needles of the bristlecone run back for a foot or more like foxtails. And the purple-tinged cones of the latter have sharp bristles at the end of each scale. The Schulman Grove, at 10,000 feet, named for the late Dr. Edward L. Schulman, a relentless investigator who determined the age of trees by microscopic study of core borings, is an almost pure stand of bristlecones, a concentration of the oldest known trees. One of two trails leads to Pine Alpha, a 4,300-year-old tree, nearly four feet across but clinging to life with only a ten-inch strip of bark and living cambium tissue. All of these trees appear at first to be dead wood, but they bear a similar strand of bark twisting around the one living side or branch. This is their way of adjusting to the limitations of moisture and soil nutrient—they retard growth to the narrow lifeline, and let erosion polish the dead branches. Another, longer trail leads to Methuselah Walk and the oldest known tree anywhere in the world. It was already well along on this spot when the Egyptians were building the pyramids, 15 centuries before Christ.

At the breeze-swept slopes 11,000 feet above sea level, the Patriarch Grove contains the largest, most contorted bristlecones, including the giant of all, the Patriarch, with a circumference of 36 feet 8 inches around its multiple stems. This great tree and others fling their bony fingers into the wind toward the mountain ranges of Nevada.

Inland and northward, the boreal forests are marked by short summers, harsh and long winters. The dense growth of firs, spruce and hemlocks are interspersed with rivers and lakes, shaping the life community. Wild geese and ducks flock to them from hundreds of miles when the climate is right in order to nest and rear their young. But when skies turn chilly and gray, the birds disappear, leaving the elk and moose to brave the snow in search of food. On the same latitudes of the West Coast, however, warm Pacific currents temper the cold. On the Olympic Peninsula, the massive Olympic Mountains intercept rain, snow and mist from the ocean winds. The combination of climate and moisture makes the western flank of this peninsula a kingdom of evergreen giants.

Similar forests parallel the Pacific Coast from Alaska to California, but none is more lush or productive than those of the Olympic valleys. The mightiest tree of this country is the Douglas fir, exceeded in size only by the California giant sequoia and coast redwood. The stately, wonderfully proportioned Douglas fir grows to heights of 250 and sometimes 300 feet. In age, the larger trees may be from 400 to 1,000 years old. For years this

*The towering saguaro cactus is the largest tree in the American desert.*

unique conifer was a botanical puzzler, having been called spruce, hemlock, balsam fir and even pine. It was discovered on Vancouver Island in 1791 by Dr. Archibald Menzies, but was named for David Douglas, the roving Scottish botanist, who carried a specimen to England for the Royal Horticultural Society.

As a timber tree, Douglas fir is probably the world's most valuable species of conifer, but in the Quinault Valley, a part of Olympic National Forest, a luxuriant rain forest community is protected. Within the densest part of the grove the parcel known as the "Big Acre" contains the greatest known stand of Douglas fir. Trees here are nearing 300 feet in height and four centuries in age, and are growing more vigorously than some youngsters half their age elsewhere.

In the morning, as dawn arrives, the trees drip with moisture. The forest is filled with soft green light and shadows and filtering shafts of warm sun. Trees, shrubs, flowering plants, giant ferns, fungi, mosses, lichens, animals and birds are all part of life in this rain forest. Some mosses grow like airplants, draped on tree limbs. Others cover dead trees on the forest floor or rocks which they will crush slowly and patiently into inorganic soil. The forest litter features a drama all its own, performed by a large company of worms, mice, shrews and salamanders in various roles intended to prepare the stage for higher forms of life. There would be no Douglas fir giants without them.

One can also see here signs of the Roosevelt or Olympic elk, the largest member of the wapiti family except for the moose. The footprints in hardened mud, teeth marks on browsed trees and shrubs, pellets over the ground, are calling cards left the previous winter before the elks' return to the high meadows. In the evening, a downy woodpecker pokes for his supper among insect larvae burrowed in the dead snags. The muted warbling of a thrush is heard from streamside. An admirable replica of the Big Acre in diorama is displayed in the Hall of North American Forests at the American Museum of Natural History in New York, but the sounds, smells, shadows and infinite varieties of life in a rain forest are well beyond man's genius to reproduce.

It happens seldom in the United States, perhaps nowhere else but the Wasatch Mountains of northern Utah. There, within a few miles of one another, in Cache National Forest, grow three massive ancient trees, each the oldest known of its kind.

The Jardine Juniper is the most celebrated example of all the Rocky Mountain junipers found between the glaciated valleys of British Columbia and the mesas of the Southwest. It stands on a rocky crag in Logan Canyon, 17 miles east of Logan, at the end of a steep trail off the road to Bear Lake astride the Utah-Idaho border. The tree was discovered in 1923 by a student of botany and plant pathology who realized that it was an extraordinary giant of a juniper. His professors later determined that it was not only large—measuring eight feet in diameter, 27 feet in circumference and 44 feet in height—but also over 3,200 years old. Thereupon it was named in honor of William M. Jardine, a former student at Logan who was Secretary of Agriculture under Calvin Coolidge, and to this day it is the goal of the annual Old Juniper Hike, sponsored by

*The beautiful prickly pear grows in many National Forests, usually in rocky or sandy places.*

*Joyce Kilmer Memorial Forest: The litter of the forest floor is a prerequisite stage for the coming of the large trees.*

Utah State University and scout troops, and well attended by tree enthusiasts

The gnarled trunk and branches are slowly dying, but the height, girth and narrow rounded crown are still impressive. The many naked limbs stripped of foliage and the hollow trunk suggest a singular story. The tree is thought to have begun life in the crevice of a limestone rock. Study of the rings shows that it grew slowly at first, with scant water and food, then much more rapidly. In the 1870's something happened, possibly a fire that exposed the topsoil to erosion; since then the growth rate of 60 rings per inch has changed to 200 per inch, which means slower growth.

Nineteen miles north in Logan Canyon a marker points the direction of the trail to the limber pine.

Firmly entrenched on an exposed rocky peak, this tree is not especially impressive to the eye. It stands 44 feet, while some limber pines in the high mountains of Arizona and New Mexico are almost twice as tall. It looks like a clump, a bushy thing with branching trunks, but all five branches actually emanate from a single trunk. This tree has been estimated to be more than 2,000 years old, much older than any other limber pine of record.

Twenty-five miles beyond, up St. Charles Canyon near Bloomington, Idaho, the champion Englemann spruce is nearly twice as tall as either the Jardine juniper or the limber pine. It measures 104 feet in height, nearly 20 feet around, and has been growing on this spot for the past 2,000 years.

The Englemann, which normally grows in the highest, coldest forest environment of the West, is a beautiful, thriving tree on this site for all its age. The deep blue-green needles are more than an inch in length. Its trunk is a straight, tapering spire with a graceful pyramidal crown of small branches. For any "collector" of trees, these three champions make this portion of the National Forest System a worthwhile goal.

When the glaciers moved south, they came as near the Appalachians as the Ohio Valley, destroying life in their paths, driving plants south in search of survival. This they found in the high mountain valleys of Appalachia, which became a haven for northern life forms, sharing the refuge with southerly species to form the mixed hardwood forest. In this condition the Indians found these valleys; so did the early settlers, and the early loggers, as well. "The forests are chiefly of hardwoods," observed a Government report on Appalachia in 1902 prepared by the Department of Agriculture and submitted to Congress by President Theodore Roosevelt. "On the drier slopes, and especially on the south sides, oak and chestnut form the greater part of the timber, with some black and yellow pine on the ridges. The timber in the hollows is more varied and the stand is heavier, poplar, birch, linn and buckeye being associated with the oak and chestnut."

Joyce Kilmer Memorial Forest, near Robbinsville, North Carolina, a portion of Nantahala National Forest, is one of the few choice examples remaining of the primeval Appalachian hardwood wilderness—the loggers took virtually all the rest during a period when the nation felt trees were superabundant. In 1934, however, the Veterans of Foreign Wars petitioned the Government for a fitting memorial to Kilmer, the author of the poem "Trees." After a nationwide survey, this tract was chosen, and today it is probably as superb as any woodland of its size on earth.

*Mount Baker National Forest: High mountain watershed country at the head of Miners Creek as seen from Suiattle Pass.*

It was pure luck that this hardwood cove has survived in its virgin condition when all the lands around it have been harvested. History records that during the lumbering era two syndicates were engaged in intensive cutting in this region. They were moving steadily toward this tract with a logging railroad. When they came within two miles both companies went bankrupt.

Within this national shrine are 100 species of hardwood trees. Patriarchs five and six centuries old form a procession of almost unending arboreal diversity. They are immense fellows, some measuring 20 feet in circumference and standing 150 feet tall, a rare collection showing what the past was like in sheltered coves throughout the hills.

Along the trail one sees sycamore, oaks, birch, walnut, maples, basswood, cherry and buckeye. Each tree has a personality and usefulness of its own. The yellow poplar, or tulip tree, one of the tallest, bears tulip-shaped leaves. Its large greenish-yellow flowers are among the early spring arrivals, a welcome source of nectar to honeybees. The beech is another giant, clothed in a silvery gray smooth bark with pear-shaped, straight-veined leaves. The beech yields to wildlife its edible sweet-meated nuts—just when the animals need them, before the coming of winter. The missing member of the forest, unfortunately, is the chestnut, which ranged throughout the Appalachian forest before being struck down by the mysterious blight that arrived from Asia. Many foresters regarded it as the finest hardwood tree in America. Its nuts were a food staple of squirrels, turkeys, bears and other animals, and the entire forest environment suffered when the chestnut passed.

Far below the crown of the ancient forest on the carpet of deep soil grow smaller trees and shrubs and a myriad of humble plants and herbs. The birdfoot violet brings the touch of lilac color to forest springtime. The bloodroot, a delicate plant of the poppy family, blooms with a large flower of white or pink petals, while its underground stem contains a juice as bright and red as blood. On the arching stalk of the delicate Dutchman's-breeches, finely drawn petals expand into spurs like a pair of bright breeches tipped with yellow. The evergreen walking fern, or "sore eye," a strange ancient plant growing over the moist, mossy rocks, spawns offspring when the tips of its finely tapered fronds touch the ground.

There are dozens of other important forest associations in the National Forests worthy of study and appreciation—the Southern pines, hardwood-conifer mixtures of New England, second growth forests and plantations in the Lake States, white pine of Idaho and the Northwest, high alpine forests, majestic redwoods of California. Each has a dramatic story to tell.

*St. Joe National Forest: Grove of Western white pine, which differ from Eastern white pine in having hairy twigs.*

Over a quarter century ago the American Forestry Association began a nationwide search to identify the largest specimens of several hundred trees. The objective was then—and remains today—to halt the tragic disappearance of important natural landmarks. These trees are found under all kinds of land ownership: National Forests, National Parks, state parks, county and city parks, college campuses, cemeteries, Indian reservations, National Wildlife Refuges, arboretums, commercial timberlands and private residential property. The 41 members of the "Social Register of Big Trees" located in National Forests are listed on the opposite page.

# Social Register of Big Trees in National Forests

| Tree | Circumference | Hgt. | Spd. | National Forest |
|------|------|------|------|------|
| Alder, white<br>*Alnus rhombifolia* | 11'3" | 93' | 45' | Angeles,<br>California |
| Aspen, quaking<br>*Populus tremuloides* | 11'6" | 70' | 70' | Santa Fe,<br>New Mexico |
| Bayberry, Pacific<br>*Myrica californica* | 4'4" | 80' | 45' | Siuslaw,<br>Oregon |
| Cedar, Incense<br>*Libocedrus decurrens* | 36'<br>16'3" | 225'<br>(tallest) | | Rogue River,<br>California<br>Umpqua,<br>Oregon |
| Cercocarpus, Curlleaf<br>*Cercocarous ledifolius* | 10'7" | 24' | 67' | Nevada,<br>Nevada |
| Cypress, Arizona<br>*Cypressus arizonica* | 17'5" | 102' | 38' | Coronado,<br>Arizona |
| Cypress, Modoc<br>*Cypressus bakeri* | 16'2" | 70' | 42' | Plumas,<br>California |
| Douglas fir, Bigcone<br>*Pseudotsuga macrocarpa* | 24' | 120' | 64' | Los Padres,<br>California |
| Fir, Noble<br>*Abies procera* | 28'4" | 278' | 47' | Gifford Pinchot,<br>Washington |
| Hemlock, Mountain<br>*Tsuga mertensiana* | 21'9" | 118' | 84' | Stanislaus,<br>California |
| Juniper, Alligator<br>*Juniperus deppeana* | 29'7" | 57' | 57' | Tonto,<br>Arizona |
| Juniper, Rocky Mountain<br>*Juniperus scopulorum* | 26'8" | 45' | | Cache,<br>Utah |
| Juniper, Western<br>*Juniperus occidentalis* | 42'9" | 87' | 51' | Stanislaus,<br>California |
| Larch, Subalpine<br>*Larix lyallis* | 13'4" | 50' | 22' | Bitterroot,<br>Montana |
| Larch, Western<br>*Larix occidentalis* | 24' | 120' | 37' | Kootenai,<br>Montana |
| Oak, Chapman<br>*Quercus chapmanii* | 4'2" | 58' | 33' | Ocala,<br>Florida |
| Oak, Gambel<br>*Quercus gambelii* | 18'3" | 47' | 85' | Gila,<br>New Mexico |
| Oak, Canyon Live<br>*Quercus chrysolepis* | 32'5" | 67' | 109' | Stanislaus,<br>California |
| Oak, Oracle<br>*Quercus xmoreha* | 8'8" | 30' | 40' | San Bernardino,<br>California |
| Oak, Turkey<br>*Quercus laevis* | 8' | 63' | 50' | Ocala,<br>Florida |
| Oak, Oregon White<br>*Quercus garryana* | 25'6" | 120' | | Mendocino,<br>California |
| Pine, Bristlecone<br>*Pinus aristata* | 37'7" | 40' | 45' | Inyo,<br>California |
| Pine, Coulter<br>*Pinus coulterii* | 17' | 144' | 40' | Angeles,<br>California |
| Pine, Foxtail<br>*Pinus balfouriana* | 22'10" | 35' | 20' | Inyo,<br>California |
| Pine, Jack<br>*Pinus banksiana* | 6'6" | 91' | 21' | Superior,<br>Minnesota |
| Pine, Jeffrey<br>*Pinus jeffreyii* | 20'3" | 197' | 54' | Sierra,<br>California |
| Pine, Knobcone<br>*Pinus attenuata* | 10'4" | 98' | 43' | Sierra,<br>California |
| Pine, Limber<br>*Pinus flexilis* | 24'5" | 44' | 50' | Cache,<br>Utah |
| Pine, Lodgepole<br>*Pinus contorta* | 19'8" | 110' | 37' | San Bernardino,<br>California |
| Pine, Pinyon<br>*Pinus edulis* | 11'3" | 33' | 44' | Manti-La Sal,<br>Utah |
| Pine, Ponderosa<br>*Pinus ponderosa* (tallest) | 14'11" | 246' | | Siskiyou,<br>Oregon |
| Pine, Sand<br>*Pinus clausa* | 6'11" | 91' | 36' | Ocala,<br>Florida |
| Pine, Slash<br>*Pinus eilliotti* | 10'5" | 119' | 41' | Apalachicola,<br>Florida |
| Plum, Inch<br>*Prunus americana lanata* | 1'10" | 26' | 24' | Ouachita,<br>Arkansas |
| Prickly-Ash<br>*Zanthoxylum americanum* | 1'4" | 30' | | Homochitto,<br>Mississippi |
| Rhododendron, Rosebay<br>*Rhododendron maximum* | 4'9" | 18' | 18' | Nantahala,<br>North Carolina |
| Spruce, Black<br>*Picea mariana* | 11'9" | 75' | 18' | Superior,<br>Minnesota |
| Spruce, Blue<br>*Picea pungens* | 15'8" | 126' | 36' | Gunnison,<br>Colorado |
| Spruce, Brewer<br>*Picea breweriana* | 13'8" | 170' | 39' | Siskiyou,<br>Oregon |
| Spruce, Englemann<br>*Picea englemannii* | 20'7" | 140' | 34' | Willamette,<br>Oregon |
| Spruce, White<br>*Picea glauca* | 10'6" | 116' | 27' | Superior,<br>Minnesota |

# II | The Wilderness: A National Treasure

**M**an cannot cast his shadow on the rising of the sun, or halt the flow of the winds, or alter the rhythm of the waves. But he can enrich his humanity with appreciation of the greater world that lies above and beyond his own.

Wilderness is the tangible essence of the greater world placed within our grasp to touch and feel, and to test our sensitivity.

When the Wilderness Law was adopted in 1964, declaring wilderness a valuable national resource in itself, America affirmed faith in its destiny and in the continuum of its yesterdays and tomorrows. For wilderness always has been, and always will be, part of the search for truth, as well as part of man's desire to know himself and the source of his creation.

"In wildness I sense the miracle of life, and beside it our scientific accomplishments fade to trivia," wrote Charles A. Lindbergh, whose own life epitomizes the age of great scientific accomplishment. "The construction of an analogue computer or a supersonic airplane is simple when compared to the mixture of space and evolutionary eons represented by a cell. In primitive rather than in civilized surroundings I grow aware of man's evolving status, as though I were suddenly released from a hypnotic state. Life itself becomes the standard of all judgment. How could I have overlooked, even momentarily, such an obvious fact?"

The awareness of John Bartram, explorer of the 18th-century wilderness, and the first great naturalist born in English America, was much less clouded by man's meager creations and therefore he never overlooked the "obvious fact" of life. "My head runs all upon the works of God, in nature," he wrote two centuries before Lindbergh. "It is through that telescope I see God in his glory."

*View of northwest slopes of Oregon's Mount Jefferson which gives its name to a primitive area located here.*

Thus, the further we move away from the natural ways of our ancestors, the further we move into urbanized insulation, the further rising populations advance across the natural domain, so the slender primeval places become more priceless as fountains of sustenance and renewal to the soul.

The magic of wilderness is many things to many people. To the ghetto dweller, it may be compressed into the sight of a blade of grass. To a suburbanite, it may be the perfume of honeysuckle in a woodland not yet subdivided, to the farmer it may be the fragrance of an open field after a spring shower.

In the National Forest System, lands designated for wilderness management and protection as wilderness are still expansive, covering approximately 14 million acres. They are located on portions of 73 National Forests in 14 states, extending from the mountains of New England and the southern Appalachians to most regions of the West.

In wilderness no mechanized equipment is permitted (except in emergency and when necessary for administration). Trees are not cut, nor permanent roads built. Virtually all developments except trails and shelters—simple facilities necessary to allow use without damaging the wilderness resource—are prohibited. The emphasis is on keeping (and restoring) wilderness in its natural state for those who journey beyond civilization.

Wilderness is an integral part of multiple-use management.

It helps in the protection of watersheds, the storage and production of water.

*Emigrant Basin Primitive Area in California's Stanislaus National Forest displays in abundance those qualities that make the wilderness an important resource.*

*Sawtooth Wilderness Area: Ridge on north side of Mount Cramer shows Arrowhead Rock just to the right of center.*

It offers refuge and roving room to big animals who might otherwise be lost, including the grizzly bear, mountain lion, mountain goat and elk, as well as deer, fur bearers, birds and small creatures. It furnishes sportsmen opportunities for some of the most challenging hunting on this continent and for fishing in clear, free-flowing streams and lakes carved out of the earth by its own forces.

As a scientific resource, it serves as a living laboratory, a control plot, where the biologist, botanist, ornithologist and ecologist can measure the behavior of plants free of human intervention. From such observations have come advancements in medical science, sources of new foods to cultivate and commercial products useful to man.

Wilderness is a many-sided recreational resource. Some come to travel the long trails, others to climb the ancient mountains, to camp in the fullness of night, to exercise the body and stimulate the mind, to contemplate the shape and substance of wildflowers, to follow the arc of the eagle, to luxuriate in solitude, to feel the summons of adventurous times.

Almost everybody uses wilderness in one way or another. The family that camps in a developed area nearby feels it as a warm and welcome neighbor, an unscarred scenic backdrop. The motoring family sees it as a sweeping vista on the landscape. The airplane passenger can look down and tell that the varied physiography of the land is not all cleft and carved from the same standard mechanical patterns. The person who stays at home and goes nowhere can know that a fragment of the original America still endures for the benefit of pioneers unborn.

The idea of protecting wilderness arose early in the history of the National Forests. Possibly the first time was in October 1919, when a group of rangers and Arthur Carhart, the first landscape architect employed by the Forest Service, met at the shore of Trappers Lake, in White River National Forest, Colorado. Their assigned mission was to choose a location for a projected cluster of summer homes, to be reached by road. After due discussion and debate, they failed completely, deciding there should be no cluster and no summer homes to mar the beauty spot of the high Rockies. The regional forester concurred, adding that there should be no road either.

In those years Aldo Leopold was thinking about the future of National Forest wilderness in the Southwest. He proposed in detail a new kind of management plan. Logging would be restricted to the richest, most accessible—and therefore most economical—forested regions, while the balance would be reserved for various forms of recreation, game management and wilderness. Under his leadership, a 500,000-acre area embracing the hazy Mogollon Mountains in Gila National Forest became, in 1924, the first Federal land designated for wilderness preservation. During the same period Arthur Carhart arrived at the Superior National Forest in Minnesota with an assignment to lay out a recreational development of roads and lakeshore summer home sites. But he discovered other values: that the area could be "as priceless as Yellowstone, Yosemite or the Grand Canyon—if it remained a water-trail wilderness." He fought for this objective and the establishment of the Superior Primitive Area, later to become the Boundary Waters Canoe Area, renowned the world over because it remains roadless.

In 1929, the first specific procedures for wilderness designation were spelled out, laying the basis for surveying and classifying millions of acres. Under subsequent modification and refinement, public hearings were required before a wilderness area could be established, modified or eliminated by the Secretary of Agriculture on the recommendation of the Chief of the Forest Service.

In 1964, however, the United States became the first nation in the long history of civilization to proclaim through legislation a recognition of wilderness as part of its culture and its legacy to the future. The adoption that year of the Wilderness Law, providing for the establishment of a National Wilderness Preservation System, reinforced the feeling for nature that is deeply rooted in the national conscience.

The Wilderness System may in time comprise 50 million acres of wildland—totalling no more than two or three per cent of the entire surface of the country—including portions of National Parks and National Wildlife Refuges, as well as the National Forests. These units will continue to be administered by the separate agencies. The system became a reality with the Wilderness Law itself; it designated for inclusion all areas of the National Forests previously classified as "Wild," "Wilderness," or "Canoe," covering more than nine million acres.

This law also provides for study over a ten-year period of lands classified as National Forest Primitive Areas under the old regulations, and of all qualified additional areas under jurisdiction of the other two agencies. These may be added to the system based on reports of the Secretaries of Agriculture and Interior

*Some sticky jumping cholla cactus along a trail in the Superstition Mountains of Tonto National Forest.*

*Left: The wilderness is many things to many people, from the awesome sight of a grizzly to a glimpse of a butterfly.*

to the President and recommendations of the President to Congress. Additions to the system become effective when approved by an act of Congress. Above all, this law challenges the people. Before additions, deletions or changes are made in the Wilderness System, these must be aired and discussed at public hearings and the public must be heard.

What sort of lands are protected in wilderness?

According to the letter of the law, they must generally appear to have been affected primarily by the forces of nature, with the imprint of man's work substantially unnoticeable. They must have outstanding opportunities for solitude or a primitive and unconfined type of recreation. They may also contain ecological, geological, or other features of scientific, educational, scenic or historical value.

As one views the wilderness units of the National Forests, he sees that they are national documents inscribed in the land. They embrace the range of life communities from desert to brushland through the alpine to the glacial. Each one tells a different story.

For example:

Bob Marshall Wilderness in Montana includes the "Chinese Wall," a 15-mile-long escarpment which rises vertically for 1,000 feet in sheer cliffs. The spectacular wall is part of the Lewis Overthrust, a major geological feature of the Rocky Mountains. Mountain goats often are spotted on narrow ledges of the cliff face. Covering over one million acres of the Flathead and Lewis and Clark National Forests, the Bob Marshall Wilderness contains long stretches of wild rivers, a variety of forests, grassy slopes and wildflower-covered meadows. The Wilderness is popular in summer for hiking, trail riding, trout fishing and camping, and in fall for choice hunting. Bob Marshall, for whom it is named, was a vigorous pioneer of National Forest wilderness protection, who loved this particular area.

Great Gulf Wilderness offers a retreat into solitude and beauty in the heart of the White Mountain National Forest in New Hampshire. The narrow, steep-sided "gulf," with gradual, broadening base, is actually a glacial valley further carved by harsh, tormenting winds. Great Gulf, though, with 5,400 acres, the smallest National Forest Wilderness, attracts many hikers following the trails from the valley floor at 1,700 feet to 5,800 feet, near the summit of Mount Washington. The trails pass lovely cascades tumbling downward to the Peabody River, forests of spruce and fir, and alpine flora on the upper reaches. Two shelters with fireplaces are maintained by the Appalachian Mountain Club. The Wilderness forms part of the view from the Mt. Washington Auto Road.

*(Continued on page 47)*

*Uncompahgre National Forest: Unaweep Canyon is an ancient channel for a river that no longer exists.*

Glen Lake in Michigan's Ottawa National Forest
displays beauty and solitude of northwoods.

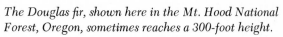

The Douglas fir, shown here in the Mt. Hood National
Forest, Oregon, sometimes reaches a 300-foot height.

*View from overlook near John Muir Trail in unrivalled High Sierra Wilderness Area in California.*

*Rugged Uinta Canyon Gorge is typical of High Uintas Wilderness Area, Ashley National Forest, Utah.*

*Maroon Bells towers behind lake in a striking wilderness area
of Colorado's White River National Forest.*

The High Uintas Primitive Area of eastern Utah covers the major mountain range of the country running along an east-west axis, instead of the usual north-south, and the highest peaks of Utah, rising over 13,000 feet. Over a quarter million acres of the Ashley and Wasatch National Forests have been protected and managed as wilderness since 1931. The Uintas, with broad high basins and purple canyon walls, are noted for hiking and mountain climbing, as well as for fishing. These mountains, as Professor Walter P. Cottam of the University of Utah has said, are too close to heaven ever to have served as Robber's Roost, too close to winter to make livestock grazing a sustained lucrative business, too poor in mineral wealth to lure the miner, too rugged to shelter, for long, weak flesh—either man or beast. The High Uintas are richly endowed in only three basic resource values—water, scientific research, recreation. And if the last two are protected, the first is bound to be protected, too.

Kalmiopsis Wilderness, in the Cascade Mountains of southern Oregon, is a botanist's paradise, devoted to providing sanctuary to a shrub, one of the rarest in the world. The kalmiopsis, somewhat resembling a delicate rhododendron, is a relic of the Tertiary Age and one of the three oldest members of the heath family. It grows among outcrops of weathered periodotite rocks, which give a reddish color to the higher peaks. The Wilderness covers 78,000 acres of the Siskiyou National Forest and is noteworthy for the variety of floral species. Among the rare and unusual plants are several species of orchids, gentians, the curious darlingtonia, and strange members of the lily family.

In such wildlands man himself is the visitor who does not remain.

Until our time they required little management because they were remote and little used. Now, with rising popularity, they must have careful protection to guard against overuse and misuse. At some areas the number of visitors may have to be regulated.

Nevertheless, for all those who enter its portals, for as short as a day, or even for a fleeting hour, wilderness provides a quality of enjoyment and refreshment found nowhere else. One can walk only 100 yards to feel the unconquered land that once possessed America. Here even invalids can thrill to the rare wonder and beauty. It isn't how much distance one covers, but what he perceives—slowness, indeed, expands the dimensions of time; it encourages one to absorb the fullness of what lies close at hand. So wilderness touches the heart, mind and soul of each individual in a way known only to himself.

*Bob Marshall Wilderness Area: Looking south along the east face of the "Chinese Wall," a 15-mile-long escarpment.*

# III | Scenic Roads—
# Quiet Alternative to Freeways

*Let the eye at this living instant survey from a
    vantage point
The swelling majesty of our mountains and
    their infolded peace,
And take in the rich greenery and warm heath
    of the forest
And note how, holding time in suspense,
They absorb all sound into silence, all move-
    ment into the trance of stone.*

—*From* Rothiemurchus,
    *by the English poet, William Jeffrey*

Motoring, it is often reported, has become the nation's most popular form of outdoor recreation. This may be, but in the National Forests motoring is not designed as the end in itself, nor as mere transportation, but rather as the vantage point from which to observe the swelling majesty of mountains. And the road itself is the gateway from which to enter, on foot, the rich greenery and warm heath of the forest.

Scenic roads lace the National Forests. They are for driving awhile and stopping awhile, at overlooks, campgrounds, areas of special scenic or historic interest, and at the start of footpaths. They provide a refuge for the genuine motoring tourist, who prefers a leisurely tempo, free of congestion, and a chance to break away from the monotony of long stretches of concrete and asphalt, which may be landscaped only with billboards.

In the National Forests, road landscaping depends on season and setting. Given spring in Virginia, the Carolinas, Tennessee or Georgia, it will be dogwood and wildflowers in April, followed by mountain laurel, flame azalea and rhododendron. Above timberline in the West it will be a mass of snow glistening in the

*Left: Northward view from Cape Perpetua on the Oregon Coast, one of the nation's outstanding scenic areas.*

bright sunlight. On the Mather Memorial Parkway, running through the White River Valley in Snoqualmie National Forest of Washington State, the landscaping is furnished by towering and somber Douglas fir trees— this is a boulevard of giants, a worthy tribute to Stephen T. Mather, pioneer of National Parks.

Across Puget Sound, Route 101, the Olympic Highway, encircles the Olympic Peninsula, with many campgrounds and scenic areas of the Olympic National Forest along the way. Anyone who works up an appetite while driving along the Hood Canal can take time out at the Seal Rock Campground to dig a few clams and oysters out of the sand, or simply to enjoy the cool setting where the forest dips down to the water's edge. The motorist towing a boat can launch it from the dock and look up toward the glistening Olympics from the middle of the canal, a finger of Puget Sound.

On drives off the Olympic Highway the visitor can perceive the beauty and fertility of this corner of Washington State. Mount Walker Summit, reached by road near Quilcene, looks deep into forested ridges and valleys, as well as off to Juan de Fuca Strait and the distant Cascades. Then there are drives into the green recesses along the Dosewallips, Duckabush and Hamma Hamma Rivers, which derive their names from the Indian tongues.

Many roads lead into high country. The motorist who loses interest and grows drowsy on a turnpike will never become weary climbing the flanks and passes of the Appalachians, Ozarks, Black Hills, Rocky Mountains, the Sierras, Cascades or Coast Range.

In Colorado, roads, like mountains, seem to come nearest to the sky. The highest in the country rises from Idaho Springs up through the walls of Chicago Creek Canyon and Arapaho National Forest. Fir, pine and spruce yield to rock and tundra, colored with high alpine wildflowers. The final climb begins from Echo Lake, at 10,600 feet, but the grade does not exceed six per cent. From the 14,259-foot summit, the Great Plains are visible for more than a hundred miles spreading eastward. The entire Front Range is in view, a mass of snowy peaks, glaciers, silvery streams and rock walls rising above the forests.

Across the state, on the western slope of the Rockies, the Million Dollar Highway runs through the mining district of the San Juan National Forest. At one end lies Ouray, sheltered like a Swiss village by 14,000-foot peaks. For 23 miles the highway winds through tortuous canyons, over a surface of gold-bearing gravel (from which it gets its name), crossing waterfalls and bending around pyramid-shaped Mount Adams before finally emerging at Silverton.

Few roads in the United States match the scenic splendor of the Beartooth Highway through the Custer, Gallatin and Shoshone National Forests. From many points along the 64-mile route between Cooke City and Red Lodge, Montana, the traveler can look across vast unbroken stretches of primitive America, embraced within the Beartooth Wilderness and Absaroka Wilderness. More than 25 peaks rise above 12,000 feet,

including Granite Peak, the highest in Montana. The Nez Percé Indians crossed this way centuries before the white man and called it "path above the eagles."

Campgrounds are located on streams along the way, each with its own forest environment for outdoor recreation. The highway is lined with viewpoints offering a short course in geology—and therefore a deeper than eye-level appreciation of the American earth. The rocks exposed along the road become perceivable as metamorphosed gneisses, schists and quartzites, among the oldest known to man. The small, common cirque lakes become recognizable as the basins of rock-walled amphitheatres carved into the heads of valleys by glacial action, and the moraines, characterized by large boulders, as the remnants left by melting glaciers within the past million years.

Beartooth Lake, at 9,000 feet, is a favorite spot with

*Coronado National Forest, Arizona: Rock formation resembling knight's helmet can be seen near a road going up Mount Lemmon.*

*Eldorado National Forest, California: Snow-cat on State Highway 88 shows one way of enjoying winter scenery in rugged country.*

trout fishermen, hikers, photographers and viewers of Beartooth Butte, a mass of sedimentary rock deposited by an ancient sea. Trips into the back country are available from the lodge here, as well as from motels, dude ranches and outfitters in the valleys below. A one-day excursion by jeep and foot leads to Grasshopper Glacier in the Beartooth Wilderness, twelve miles north of Cooke City, so named for the presence of millions of grasshoppers frozen in the ice about 200 years ago. Thus, the scenic road really is a corridor linked to a much larger recreational complex.

The Lewis and Clark Highway is another such case. It extends 133 miles through Lolo and Clearwater National Forests between Lolo, Montana, and Kooskia, Idaho, flanking the Selway-Bitterroot Wilderness and some of the most impressive mountain scenery in the Northwest. It generally follows or parallels the 1805-06 trail of Lewis and Clark along the Lochsa River through Lolo Pass, the ancient route used by the Nez Percé in hunting buffalo. Markers identify the settings of events recorded by Lewis and Clark during their harrowing adventure over the Bitterroots. Heading west, they found the Bitterroots to be the most trying obstacle of their entire expedition—worn with despair, fatigue and hunger, they were forced to subsist on horsemeat and very nearly called off the whole trek.

The Lewis and Clark Highway is a record of history.

It is also the entranceway to campgrounds in forests of pine, fir, cedar and larch, and to hiking trails above deep canyons and streams, including some with choice trout fishing. It is not unusual to spot elk around natural salt licks, or moose, bear, or mountain goat, for the Selway-Bitterroot is a refuge for them all.

Driving south of Lolo through the Bitterroot Valley, the main road, Route 93, follows a course within sight of National Forests for many miles. Fort Owen State Monument at Stevensville tells the story of St. Mary's Mission, the oldest in the Northwest, established in 1841 by pioneering Father Pierre-Jean de Smet at a time when the Flathead tribe occupied the valley. It was the beginning of the first permanent white settlement in Montana. Hamilton, the center of the valley, flanked by the high peaks of the Bitterroots and the Sapphire Mountains, is headquarters of the Bitterroot National Forest, a source of directions for scenic drives. One possibility is the Bitterroot Wildflower Area, where many wildflowers are identified by signs; choice among these is the pinkish spring blooming state flower, the bitterroot, which now grows only in western Montana and in the gravel terraces between Boyd and Red Lodge. Another possibility is the drive to a special forestry landmark, the restored first ranger station built in this region over 60 years ago, at the old gold camp of Alta, on the west fork of the Bitterroot River.

51

The motorist searching for high adventure, however, will turn east into the Sapphires. This spectacular drive, much less known than the Beartooth or Lewis and Clark Highways, leads up to Skalkaho Pass, elevation 7,258 feet, near the corner of the Anaconda-Pintlar Wilderness, surrounded by lofty peaks, and with an easy walk to Skalkaho Falls, one of the prettiest cascades in Montana. From Porters Corner, at Georgetown Lake, the motorist can turn north through the Deerlodge National Forest and the old silver and gold country, where Montana's first strike was made in 1852. Phillipsburg was the scene of the first silver mill in the state (and also doubled as a fort for protection from Indians). One mile away, the ghost camp at Granite Mountain was once called the greatest silver producer of all, the richest on earth.

The West still has such spacious places where wildlife species are more numerous than people. In New England, a tight little region, turnpikes and freeways have brought the remotest corners to within a few hours of the dwellers of metropolitan centers who have a desperate need and urge for space and natural ways. To them the Kancamagus Highway in White Mountain National Forest, the largest parcel of public land in New England, fills somewhat the same role as the Beartooth and Lewis and Clark Highways. It extends 34 miles between Lincoln and Conway through the heart of the White Mountains, alongside streams and wooded peaks. The most unusual facility along the way, Covered Bridge Campground, on the Swift River, is named for the only covered bridge currently protected by the Federal Government—it simply was there before the National Forest and the motor car. There also are scenic areas preserving undisturbed beauty: Sabbaday Falls, reached on a five-minute walk, and Greeley Ponds and Rocky Gorge, involving longer climbs. The whole Kancamagus Highway is a blaze of color in autumn, and in winter the Loon Mountain development becomes part of the New England ski scene.

*Black Hills National Forest: Impressive view of Mount Rushmore from switchback on Iron Mountain Road.*

*The fast-flowing Uncompahgre River runs beside U.S. Highway 550 north of Ouray, Colorado.*

In the Southern highlands, the Unaka Mountain Auto Tour, starting at the Rock Creek Recreation Area in Cherokee National Forest, near Unicoi and Erwin, Tennessee, covers some of the finest scenery and unusual plant life in Appalachia. The 31-mile loop tour is designed to take about three hours, but it can easily span a full day, with time for hiking on trails of various length, including the Appalachian Trail, which twice crosses the scenic road.

Eight stops are marked along the way. The first, Indian Grave Gap, was named for a skirmish in the 1700's between settlers and Indians and the tradition that some of the latter were buried nearby. In this section, the Tennessee and North Carolina state line follows the mountaintop, as it does in the nearby Great Smokies, also a part of the massive Unaka chain west of the Blue Ridge. Standing on the crest, the visitor can be in two states and two National Forests, the Cherokee of Tennessee and Pisgah of North Carolina. Another stop borders a wildlife trail, where deer are sometimes seen. The forest is managed to sustain food and cover for the wildlife community and regulated hunting seasons in the fall help keep the deer population within the carrying capacity of the land.

The Beauty Spot is an old name, given by the mountaineers long before the National Forest was born, to a section of grassy "balds" lacking in trees and shrubs. The balds have been variously attributed to ancient tramping of buffalo from the valleys, cattle grazing by early settlers and severe forest fires. Whatever the reason, Beauty Spot is aptly named. Another stop, the Unaka Mountain Overlook, over 5,000 feet, is one of the high points of Appalachia. A rugged three-mile trail leads through some of the last remaining virgin spruce in the Eastern mountains to Horse Hump Ridge. But one can also take an easier and interesting 30-minute walk, the Raven's Lore, following the path of the bird that is often seen near Unaka Mountain.

(*Continued on page 59*)

*Northwoods' fall colors are impressive near entrance to Snap Jack Lake in the Ottawa National Forest.*

*Dazzling color makes autumn
an especially beautiful time of year
in Superior National Forest.*

*Bush-like rhododendron
plant may vary from a few inches in
height to in excess of 50 feet.*

*Superior National Forest is known for its 5,000 lakes,
but it also has a million acres of virgin timber.*

*Timber access road winds its way through old-growth
fir in Oregon's Winema National Forest.*

Red rock formations near
Echo Amphitheatre in the Carson
National Forest, New Mexico.

Montana's "big sky" country
as seen from Beartooth Highway in
Custer National Forest.

An outstanding new route, the Talimena Scenic Drive through Ouachita (pronounced WASH-i-taw) National Forest, winds 55 miles across the crests of Rich and Winding Stair Mountains from Mena, Arkansas, to Talihina, Arkansas. The Ouachitas run east and west, rather than in the north-south direction of most American ranges. The drive will utilize the forested mountain setting in providing 44 recreation areas in the south-central part of the country.

These popular and publicized scenic roads of the National Forests may not even be the very best, at least not best for the curious type of tourist who drives in order to stop and see and walk. But for him there are plenty of other roads with numbers instead of names, and sometimes not even numbers, in every National Forest and National Grassland. They are the special roads where he can hold time in suspension and absorb all sound into silence.

*Above: Campers in one of the Ottawa National Forest's many developed campgrounds preparing their evening meal.*

*Below: Switchbacks of U.S. Highway 64 in Nantahala National Forest traverse scenic mountain country. This is headwaters area for Little Tennessee River.*

*The bald eagle, a national symbol, is one of many species found in the National Forests which are in danger of extinction.*

# IV | The Fragile World
# of Endangered Wildlife

The humanitarian philosopher and the true natural scientist are given to viewing the world through the same eye, and the eye is fastened on life.

Ralph Waldo Emerson wrote that all the creatures he observed were friendly and sacred. Every chemical substance, every animal in its growth, taught him the unity of cause, that only appearances varied.

Albert Schweitzer commented that a man is ethical when life becomes sacred to him—not simply his own, but life as such, that of plants and animals, as well as human life—and when he devotes himself to helping life forms in need of help.

As a pioneer in the science of game management, based on ecological balance, Aldo Leopold felt that the administration of National Forests has for its real purpose the perpetuation of all life: human, plant and animal.

"Of first importance is human life," wrote Leopold, "and so close is this to tree and plant life, so vital are the influences of the forest, that their problems have been fashioned into major problems of forest management and administration.

"Of next importance, and ever increasing, is the problem of animal and bird life. Driven from their once great range by civilization, the wildlife that was at one time America's most picturesque heritage has found refuge in the National Forests."

In 1966 Congress enacted the Rare and Endangered Species Law, declaring a national policy to protect species of native fish and wildlife threatened with extinction, and to protect their habitat as well. This law reflects a sense of urgency and concern by the American people that no portion of the nation's wildlife heritage—whether mammals, birds, reptiles, amphibians or fish—should be lost to future generations.

Of 130 species classified as rare, endangered or unique by their scarcity, about 25 are known to occur in National Forests and National Grasslands. In fulfillment of responsibility under the law, priority of management is directed to the rare and endangered species, where they are presently, where they can be, and especially where they have been. It is a cooperative responsibility, shared with state fish and game departments, but the protection and enhancement of the habitat is the prime responsibility of the National Forest administration.

Preservation and numbers of any species depend directly on the condition and extent of its habitat. A given acreage will support only a certain number of animals, for nature rules that no wildlife population can survive for long above the levels of available food, cover, water and other essentials.

One unique habitat is the Rock Creek Bird Nesting Area, of 640 acres, located at 9,500 feet in Arapaho National Forest, Colorado. It consists of a 65-acre mountain open park growing a variety of grasses, willows and shrubs, surrounded by fringes of aspen, spruce and lodgepole pine. A hanging valley to the west provides alpine vegetation. In this small but diverse habitat over 60 species of birds have been sighted, including thrushes, wrens, warblers, hummingbirds, ptarmigan, hawks and golden eagles. Protection of the habitat is the prime objective of forest management.

The habitat in Chippewa National Forest, at the headwaters of the Mississippi River in northern Minnesota, makes the region one of the most important breeding areas of the bald eagle anywhere in the United States. Water is abundant, with 1,200 lakes and 155 named streams, plus innumerable marshes and swamps, and dense stands of trees, particularly mature red and white pine, the kind of community that eagles favor.

The eagle family builds its nest atop a tall tree high above a marsh within view of a river. Being big birds, they must have a big house, at least five feet across and ten feet deep, sometimes even twice that size. The eagles use mostly sticks and grass in construction, returning again and again to the same site over the years, adding new materials each year, building a bigger and better penthouse. The known number of nests at last count totals 132, including 49 considered to be active, and there probably are others.

But nesting success is low and desertion occurs on many of the active nests. In the most recent count, only 21 nests produced eaglets. It is part of the national pattern of severe decline in bald eagle numbers. An estimated 4,000 bald eagles are all that remain in the lower 48 states. An examination of nests reveals poor reproductive success everywhere. There is concern over the eagle's future as a species.

*Two male elk in a playful moment during winter in Teton National Forest, Wyoming, where thousands of elk live.*

In 1961, the National Audubon Society initiated the Continental Bald Eagle Survey in order to obtain a positive count of the current population, to investigate the cause of the decline, and to recommend measures for its adequate and lasting protection. It is already well known that residues of DDT are present in infertile eggs, picked up from fish food, and that every major river system is afflicted with pesticide residues in its channels. They may not affect the fish, but they affect the eagle. Other factors, such as human disturbance of the nests and illegal killing of the protected eagle, also are responsible for the population decline.

Eagle studies in the Chippewa National Forest are part of the Continental Project; they are also part of the multiple-use program. The first intensive efforts to locate and observe eagle nests were made in 1963, with field personnel, working from eight ranger districts, aided by game wardens, resort owners and local residents. Nests were checked first in April for signs of nesting activity. Then they were checked again in early summer to determine if young were present and the nesting successful.

The National Forest maintains a continuing inventory of nest locations as part of its resource activities. It protects the nest trees from timber cutting and all development, with a 660-foot buffer zone around each tree. Old growth trees are saved as potential nesting and roosting sites.

The inventory has shown a decided preference among the eagles for mature pine trees, a slight preference for marsh and swamp edges, particularly cedar swamps. But many questions are still unanswered. What are the significant factors in adult mortality? Where do the eagles spend the winter? What are the ecological factors in selection of a nest site—and what relation does it have to management of tree species? Above all, will the answers be learned and appropriate action taken before the eagle, the emblem of strength, courage and freedom, soars over the land on its final flight?

It is life or death for rare birds, even rarer than the eagle, huddled in the twilight of their tribes in unique habitats of the National Forests and Michigan State Forests, in which their particular forms evolved. The basis of protection and management are preservation of the species themselves, without regard to any potential economic importance.

In the case of the Kirtland's warbler, a lemon-breasted little songster weighing about half an ounce (Roger Tory Peterson calls it "butterfly of the bird world"), the first recorded observation was made by the famous Ohio naturalist, Dr. Jared Kirtland, in 1851. But its nesting ground in Michigan, near the town of Mio in what is now Huron National Forest, went undiscovered for more than 50 years. And there it was in a large tract of scrawny jack-pine, which had been swept by fire.

Study of the warbler has shown that it nests in the dry, desolate jack-pine forest and nowhere else, sheltered by young jack-pines whose lower branches reach down to touch the ground. Here it sings a low pitched, persistent and emphatic song, heard for more than a quarter of a mile on a clear day.

The cones of jack-pines, as it happens, open only as a result of intense heat, such as fire. Years ago fire was a common thing, caused by lightning and by slash burning in the wake of logging. But in the era of prevention and the spread of Smokey Bear's gospel, the fire hazard in this region of Michigan has diminished; jack-pine cones remained unopen for years on the forest floor or in the trees, and there was no new growth to provide nesting sites.

In 1963, the Huron National Forest, cooperating with the National Audubon Society, set aside a 4,000-acre tract specifically for the Kirtland's warbler, complementing similar actions already taken by the state. Instead of preventing fires, here fires are set. Every five

years another block of mature jack-pine is burned under careful control in order to assure a perpetual supply of young growth. To preclude disturbance of the nests, permits are required before entering the area; photography is not permitted. The slender tribe of warblers is still balanced on the brink—less than 100 of the birds remain. They face a long journey to and from their wintering grounds in the Bahamas, but enhancement of the specialized nesting habitat may help pull Kirtland's warblers through.

Far to the south, in Puerto Rico, about 25 miles southeast of San Juan, lies the rain forest of the Luquillo Mountains, a misty jewel of 27,500 acres now protected as the Caribbean National Forest. It includes 240 species of tropical trees—the valuable tabonuco, ausubo and laurel sabino among them—plus 50 varieties of ferns, palms, epiphytes, orchids and lichens. This woodland, with an average annual rainfall of 180 inches, is the only truly tropical forest under the U. S. flag. It is filled with the musical sound of cascading waters, the chirping of the coqui tree frog and the shrill Puerto Rican parrot, reduced to its last retreat.

*Kirtland's warbler, a lemon-breasted song bird weighing about half an ounce, has nesting ground in Huron National Forest.*

The Puerto Rican parrot belongs in the class with the whooping crane, Kirtland's warbler and California condor. It merits the same concern these better known birds have received. It is spectacular in color, emerald green over most of its 12-inch-long body, with blue wing tips, white around the eyes and reddish over the beak. Once these parrots flew in huge flocks, screeching and squawking over the forests which were widespread in Puerto Rico less than one century ago. Since then this and all the other West Indies species of *Amazona* have dwindled in numbers; adult birds have been shot for food, nestlings taken for caged pets, and the natural forest habitat has been destroyed. Numbers have declined steadily and there may be no more than 60 Puerto Rican parrots remaining. Although they live long lives, they do not lay many eggs and nesting success is very low.

In 1967 a major military maneuver involving thousands of men was planned to pass through the habitat of the parrot. Dr. Frank Wadsworth, the renowned Director of the Institute of Tropical Forestry which administers the Caribbean National Forest, succeeded in stopping it.

"Defense projects, road building and recreational development (even some types of research), all may threaten the residual parrot population," Dr. Wadsworth observed. "One of the most important Forest Service responsibilities is to see that they do not. A result has been our refusal to grant permits to 'develop' parts of the Forest, though it is inexplicable to many in the face of heavy recreational demands and pride in the progress of Puerto Rico in developing in other ways.

"The weakest link in the feeble chain which prevents this species from going over the brink is the fact that we know so little about the environmental factors, favorable and otherwise, that can be manipulated in favor of the parrots."

The birds flock together when feeding on fruits, flowers and tender shoots. They build their nests in old trees, which are preyed upon by rats. They inhabit inaccessible areas on the steep mountains and so defy study of their habits. But such a study, as Dr. Wadsworth noted, could prove the salvation of the species.

At least five rare and endangered species are found in the widely diversified types of habitat of the National Forests in California, the land of the golden bear that is no more. The rarest of the survivors are a huge bird and a little fish, demanding secure protection and skillful wildlife management.

The California condor is unsurpassed by any on this continent for the breadth of its wingspread, often extending ten feet from wingtip to wingtip. The majestic bird usually takes off from clifftops and ledges, circling into rising air currents, occasionally flapping heavily until borne aloft, then sweeping in superbly controlled flight high over jumbled ridgecrests and slopes of chaparral in the isolated reaches of Los Padres National Forest north of Los Angeles. It has keen sensitivity to locate distant carrion and is adapted to cover a vast range for food in economic flight.

Once the condor ranged all over California and into the Pacific Northwest, Mexico and as far off as Florida. Lewis and Clark reported sighting condors feeding on fish and whales when they neared the Columbia River in 1805. By 1900, however, the birds were rare, but even then many were heedlessly shot and eggs taken by curiosity seekers. Today no more than 60, possibly as few as 40, remain and the condor is considered one of the rarest living species.

*Green tree frog, one of the more common animals in the National Forest, dwells mainly in Southern states.*

*The extremely rare California condor, found in Los Padres National Forest north of Los Angeles, is a majestic bird in flight.*

In 1937 the Forest Service established the 1,200-acre Sisquoc condor sanctuary and ten years later the 53,000-acre Sespe condor sanctuary, covering an area of 16 square miles east of Ojai and Fillmore. In 1954 a state law was passed prohibiting the taking of condors for any reason. The area is patrolled by a warden of the Audubon Society, as well as the Forest Service, for the birds require total protection from human disturbance in order to assure their survival.

Sometimes they are seen, flexing tremendous wings or on a long glide over San Joaquin Valley as far as the Sierra foothills. The condor is not a predator, but feeds on carcasses of dead animals. It is still a self-reliant creature, and an inspirational one in its struggle for survival.

The Piute trout, one of the rarest, most delicately hued fish in the United States, was first observed in 1933 in the isolated waters of Silver King Creek east of the Sierra Divide in Toiyabe National Forest. From specimens collected, it was identified as a small first cousin of the Lahontan cutthroat, from which it evolved as a subspecies, but without spots on its body.

As early as 1946 efforts were made by the Forest Service and State Fish and Game Department to introduce the Piute into other mountain streams in order to insure its survival. Despite continued efforts, transplants of genetically pure stock have not been successful, for the Piute crossed and hybridized with rainbows and other cutthroats. In 1965, only 200 adult Piute remained in their own restricted range and the streams of Upper Silver Creek were closed to fishing in order to protect this slender remnant population.

Trout live in clean, cold waters—the quality of the fishery habitat is directly related to the condition of the watershed. The Silver Creek drainage on National Forest land is managed for complete streamside protection, with roads and grazing restricted. Establishment of a Piute Trout Wilderness has been considered and discussed. However, the heart of the trout habitat lies on 520 acres of private land; acquisition by the Government may be necessary to protect the drainage from such potential disturbance as mining pollution, logging, or road construction.

Why preserve a fish? For one thing, it will in time, as numbers become more secure, offer a challenge to the hardy fishermen willing to pack in for a rare catch. For another, the genetic character of the Piute may have great significance in the evolutionary formation of new subspecies, an orderly directed phenomenon of nature, furnishing a scientific and educational use of the land.

Bighorn sheep were once widespread, colorful dwellers of the high mountains and Southwestern desert with their massive permanent horns that curl a full circle or more. Since the 1850's their ranks have been decimated, not by man's progress, but largely through the mistakes associated with it. First there was overhunting in the gold rush days. Then overgrazing during the era of the cattle boom caused severe damage to the vegetation and soils, depleting the bighorn habitat. Since 1873 and the adoption of California laws protecting the bighorn, poaching and pothunting have been lingering evils, even in the 1960's.

65

Thus the history of the bighorn is one of gradual retreat. John Muir pointed out that the bighorn would be extinct, like the elk of the valleys and hills, were it not for its requirement of wilderness habitat. This it finds in rugged portions of the White and Sierra Mountains in the Inyo National Forest, where approximately 400 survive; in the towering San Gabriel Range of the San Bernardino National Forest, where an estimated 500 make their home; and in the San Gorgonio Wilderness, also part of the San Bernardino, with a remnant population of only 75.

San Gorgonio is a fascinating wilderness and the presence of bighorn is part of what makes it so. These sure-footed climbers with remarkable eyesight move across high steep cliffs, eating grassy plants, descending to lower ground only when deep snows drive them down. San Gorgonio, though only 90 miles from Los Angeles, is one of the last undeveloped mountains of southern California. The bighorns share it with over 40,000 persons yearly, who hike the trails, camp at 20 primitive sites, and climb to the summit of Mount San Gorgonio, 11,502 feet high, overlooking a megalopolis of seven million people.

Protection of the bighorn gets first priority, but present knowledge of its ecology, including the seasonal movements, the food requirements on summer and winter ranges, is still rudimentary. These need to be identified before recreational developments and trails are laid out. This may limit the movement and numbers of people, but it is necessary if the bighorn is to survive as part of the wilderness recreation they admire.

Before the gold rush, thousands of California wapiti, or dwarf elk, now known commonly as tule elk, roamed the central and coastal valleys of California. Their habitat was invaded, the elk were shot for food and fun, and they were virtually wiped out. But a few hid in the bulrushes, or tules, of the Miller and Lux cattle kingdom and when discovered were given protection by Henry Miller, the ranch boss. From that slender group the tule made their miraculous comeback and in time were transplanted to become the famous herd in Owens Valley.

The tule elk are the smallest North American elk, and the lightest in color. In Owens Valley, east of the Sierra Crest, they have lived on a 240-square mile reservation owned by the City of Los Angeles as part of its watershed system. Because of continual harassment, poaching and periodic hunts intended to keep their numbers down to 300, the elk have been wary, frightened, and seldom seen by tourists or local people.

Before 1961 it was generally thought that the animals ranged largely on the valley floor and seldom used the foothills and mountains. Then it was noticed that a portion had established themselves in the Goodale Creek area, in the eastern Sierra foothills of Inyo National Forest, sharing a range with mule deer and bighorn sheep. Habitat management has been directed to favor the big game, and livestock use, prevalent for many years, has been halted.

The position of the black-footed ferret is precarious, and its status is unknown. It may be the rarest mammal in North America. Once the ferret was found throughout the Great Plains, where its favorite food was believed to be the prairie dog. The habitat depended on the huge buffalo that grazed and trampled tall grasses, leaving succulent weeds and short grasses for the prairie dogs. Unfortunately, both the bison and "dogs" were dispatched wholesale to make way for millions of head of cattle. The relentless poisoning of prairie dogs, continuing to this day, has eliminated the main food of the ferret as well as den holes throughout most of its habitat.

The ferret, shaped like a large weasel or mink, is the mysterious figure of the wildlife world, leading a solitary life and emerging from its underground den mostly at night. In 1964 an important sighting was made by Forest Service personnel on the Buffalo Gap National Grassland in southwestern South Dakota, where a number of prairie dogs still survived, and since then efforts to restore the ferret have focused on South Dakota. However, in early 1965 a forest ranger reported seeing a black-footed ferret near Springfield, Colorado, on Comanche National Grassland. Other sightings have been reported in eastern Wyoming.

Biological knowledge concerning the natural history and ecology of the ferret is inadequate; much needs to be done to determine its range and potential numbers. But there is no doubt that any form of control directed to the prairie dog inevitably influences the ferret. Consequently a number of prairie dog towns of noteworthy size are being maintained on National Grasslands, without the blight of poison. Considering the scarcity of prairie dogs, these towns deserve to endure as valid historic documents of the Great Plains. They also fit into a program to perpetuate the short-legged, low-slung, black-pawed weasel that ferrets its way through a difficult world.

Other rare and endangered species found on lands of the National Forest System are the following:

The Kaibab squirrel, a grey-sided tree squirrel, tassel-eared with white tail, is limited to Kaibab National Forest and the north side of Grand Canyon National Park on the Kaibab Plateau. This region has probably always been the extent of its range. Dr. Joseph G. Hall, who has been studying the Kaibab squirrel for several years, reports that the population of approximately 1,000 "is now at the lowest ebb in half a century." Automobile traffic and disease are the most conspicuous causes of mortality. Measures proposed in behalf of this attractive squirrel include continued complete legal protection; management of Gambel oak and yellow pine (the Kaibab feeds on the cambium layer of these trees) to favor the squirrel, and protection against drought, disease and undue predation.

(*Continued on page 72*)

*Screech owls, which are common in all sections of the country, favor an open woods environment.*

*An elk in the Monongahela National Forest, West Virginia, which*
*also contains deer, turkey, squirrel, bear and grouse.*

*Angelina National Forest, Texas: Deer in Southern forests are often limited by amount of browse.*

*Fine alligator specimen in his favorite environment in the Ocala National Forest area, Florida.*

*American egret in Alexander Springs Recreation Area, Ocala National Forest, Florida.*

*Bighorn ram confidently surveys his rocky domain in the Arapaho National Forest, Colorado.*

*Flathead National Forest, Montana: Rocky Mountain goats inhabit the craggy heights between the forests and snow line.*

The timber wolf, the large, broad-headed wild cousin of the domestic dog, is still fairly abundant in Alaska, but virtually the last large concentration of wolves in the contiguous 48 states is found in Superior National Forest in northern Minnesota, where there are an estimated 300 to 400. An additional band, of at least 26, is protected on Isle Royale National Park in the Lake Superior portion of Michigan.

Wolves have been subject to heavy hunting and trapping pressure for bounties and to the encroachments of civilization. They are also admired for their courage and beauty. Thus, in Michigan and Minnesota a bounty is no longer paid. Whatever remnant tribe remains in the Lake Superior region of Wisconsin is completely protected. Complete protection may be necessary elsewhere, as well. Much interest has been shown in restocking wilderness areas where there would be no conflict with farmers or ranchers.

The red wolf, a small and slender animal, closely resembles the coyote, but is larger and more robust. Colors often are similar, but the tawny, or reddish element is more pronounced in the wolf and its fur is somewhat coarser. Once it was distributed across the Southern part of the country from central Texas and Oklahoma east to Georgia and Florida, and north probably to Illinois and Indiana. It is gone from most of its range, although in recent years reports of red wolves have been made in National Forests in Arkansas, Louisiana and Texas, where forest habitat suitable to the species has not been destroyed. Red wolves declined under heavy hunting and trapping pressures; also, as the coyote was heavily hunted in its normal territory in the West, it expanded its range with aggressiveness into the South, preempting terrain and mating with the wolf.

Important investigations by Dr. Douglas Pimlott have helped determine where red wolf populations exist. The Forest Service is cooperating in studying the life history and ecology of the species so that special protection measures can be instituted jointly with the states involved.

The glacier bear, grayish or bluish in color, has a restricted range in southern Alaska and northern British Columbia, where only about 500 are found. This rare bear is considered to be intimately related to the common black bear, although smaller and of a distinct color phase. It is reported to occur on National Forest land in the area of Yakutat. Glacier Bay National Monument serves as a refuge; the Alaska Board of Fish and Game has proposed regulations to give added protection by closing the bear season during July and August, and by restricting the take to one bear per person a year. No glacier bear skins may be sold.

*The California wapiti, commonly known as the tule elk, was once near extinction, now numbers about 300.*

The grizzly bear, once found all over the West and eastward to the Great Plains, is steadily declining in numbers. The last grizzly in California was reported in 1922. The total grizzly population in all states outside Alaska was estimated at about 1,100. In 1963 there were about 850, principally in Montana and Wyoming, with a few in Idaho and the San Juan Range of Colorado. The large grizzled bear, with humped shoulder and huge front claws, has learned to fear man after a history of persecution and hunting. However, varied protective measures are now being taken to reverse the trend and save the grizzly from extinction. Restrictive hunting laws or complete protection are in force in Colorado, Idaho, Montana and Alaska (the grizzly is still widespread in Alaska and actually increasing in numbers in certain areas there). Wilderness areas are most needed to assure survival of the grizzly and cessation of its persecution as a predator. The National Forests play a major role in proposals to extend complete protection for a distance of 50 miles from the boundaries of Yellowstone and Glacier National Parks, the central areas where grizzlies are found.

The trumpeter swan, a large and beautiful bird, with snowy white plumage and contrasting black bill and feet, once bred from Alaska and Arctic Canada south to Iowa and Indiana. It wintered on the estuaries of the central Atlantic states, along the gulf of Mexico, the Ohio and Mississippi River Valleys and the lower Columbia River. A generation ago the trumpeter was at the brink of extinction; although the great bird is capable of flying at speeds up to 80 miles an hour, it could not escape those who shot it in unlimited numbers for skins, feathers and meat. The comeback began in 1935 when a count showed only 73 of these birds in the contiguous United States; that year the Red Rock Lakes Migratory Waterfowl Refuge was established in southwestern Montana, cushioned from human intrusion on the north by the Beaverhead National Forest and on the south by the Targhee National Forest. The shallow lakes and marshes of the Refuge and of the Targhee in southeastern Idaho are among the principal nesting grounds of the trumpeter swan—the flocks arrive in late February and March and sing their trumpetlike mating calls. Additional breeding populations have been established by transplanting swans to Oregon, Nevada and South Dakota. They are relatively abundant on the Copper River Flats of Chugach National Forest in Alaska where they also nest. This species enjoys complete protection under the laws of the United States and Canada.

John H. Gerard from National Audubon Society

*The last concentration of timber wolves in the 48 contiguous states is in Minnesota's Superior National Forest.*

*The American bison, commonly called buffalo, is an example of a species which recovered from near extinction.*

*The black bear, the smallest and most common of American bear, inhabits several National Forests.*

The greater prairie chicken is a distinctive bird—brown, hen-like, with short, rounded tail and with the special trademark of pointed feathers on each side of the neck. It is still numerous in sections of South Dakota, Nebraska and Kansas. On much of its range, however, the tall grass prairie, its main habitat, has been transformed into croplands and grazing lands. The greater prairie chicken is found on National Grasslands of the northern prairie, where the true grasses are maintained to help meet the needs of this bird species.

The lesser prairie chicken, lighter in color and slightly smaller than the greater prairie chicken, dwells in brush-grassland prairies, and in shinnery oak and sand sagebrush of the high plains. It is very localized, and much reduced in number because of the loss of brushy grassland to agriculture. However, it still occurs on National Grasslands and surrounding areas of southwestern Kansas, southeastern Colorado, western Oklahoma and northern Texas. On the National Grasslands the needs of this game bird are fully considered in the regulation of livestock grazing.

The masked bobwhite, or quail, of Sonora, Mexico, and formerly in adjacent Arizona, is similar to the common bobwhite of the Eastern United States, but is smaller, with white patches around the eye, surrounded by black head and throat, giving a masked appearance. It is found only where grass grows thickly under desert shrubs and cactus; thus it disappeared from Arizona early in the century when the tall grass-mesquite plains were taken over by cattle grazing. The bird is rare even in Sonora, but the Levy brothers of Tucson, well-known authorities on the masked bobwhite, and Steven Gallizioli of the Arizona Game and Fish Department located a small population there. They interested the owner and the Sonora government in protecting 1,000 acres from grazing and hunting. The Forest Service is now cooperating with the State of Arizona and the Bureau of Sport Fisheries and Wildlife in attempting to reintroduce the masked bobwhite in the Coronado National Forest in selected areas south of Tucson.

The greenback cutthroat trout, a small trout rarely exceeding a pound in weight, is an original native cutthroat of the Arkansas and Platte River drainages of Colorado and Wyoming. As a result of man's intrusion into the habitat and competition from stocked trout, the little greenback has been reduced to an estimated few hundred. However, a remnant population has been found on a tributary stream in Roosevelt National Forest, and the state and the Forest Service have co-operated in transplanting the species to new waters, hoping this will help insure its survival.

The gila trout, once widespread in upper tributaries of the Gila and San Francisco Rivers of New Mexico, is now restricted to a few headwater streams in the Gila Wilderness. In order to protect this extremely fine, profusely spotted fish, the streams have been closed to fishing and to the introduction of other trout species to prevent hybridization. In the past stream improvement devices have aided the flow of water during periods of drought. Propagation and restocking in reclaimed streams near the present habitat are under study.

The Little Colorado spindace, a two- to four-inch silvery minnow, formerly found in the upper part of the Little Colorado River basin of eastern Arizona, was seriously threatened with extinction as a result of pollution and introduction of exotics and activities of man. Fewer than 1,000 were estimated in the Clear Creek drainage of Coconino National Forest, the only remaining stream where it is known to exist. Recently more of these have been found than were known before. The fish is still rare, but is not as seriously threatened as was thought a few months or a few years ago. The Forest Service and State of Arizona are endeavoring to protect the habitat to apply special management measures to the upper reaches of East Clear Creek to protect this species of fish.

The coppery-tailed elegant trogon, a colorful bird, is normally found only in old Mexico. A few pairs, however, nest in tree cavities, in the wooded canyons of the Coronado National Forest in southern Arizona. The Forest Service is coordinating habitat needs of the trogon with other uses and activities in an effort to provide maximum protection to the nesting sites.

*The magnificent grizzly bear, once found throughout the West, is declining in numbers except in Alaska.*

*Idaho's Targhee National Forest provides nesting grounds for the beautiful and rare trumpeter swan.*

# V | New Horizons in Recreation

The year after World War II an estimated 18 million visits were made by Americans to their National Forests. Within 15 years the annual total had doubled, doubled again, and then topped the 100 million mark. It was a clear case of the people discovering the values of their forests for rest, relaxation and recreation in all seasons and in many forms.

However, it was realized early in the 1960's that just serving numbers with picnic tables and camping sites could not fulfill the National Forest mission. Quantity is one thing. The quality of the experience is another.

Accordingly, the concept of a new type of management unit evolved. This is the National Recreation Area, a large and choice portion of a National Forest designated by Congress to be administered primarily for recreation. Other uses continue, but in ways that supplement and support recreation, rather than interfere with it. For instance, timber cutting might become a tool to enhance the natural landscape, or to furnish better foods for wildlife. Grazing might be employed to contribute to a pastoral and historical tableau.

As a companion to the National Recreation Area program, the Visitor Information Service was established in 1961. A more concentrated effort to reach visitors was needed as the number rose. Whether skier or fisherman or camper, each and every visitor is curious about his forest surroundings. His trip is more meaningful in almost direct proportion to what he learns and understands about the area he is visiting. Geology, more than a classroom subject, is the heartscience of the land—the movements of the raw earth over millions of years reveal themselves as the dominant force of the landscape. The Visitor Information Service is designed to aid the visitor in understanding and interpreting these movements, to "read" the lessons of the land for himself, whether in geology, biology, ecology, history or archaeology, or in the ways productive forests are managed to sustain and to renew themselves.

Museum-like visitor centers, guided walks on nature trails, self-guided trails and evening campfire programs stimulate enjoyment through understanding. They evoke the meaning of the National Forests as a cultural and scientific resource. They help to make a visit to a National Forest a truly fine experience.

Two of the new National Recreation Areas are in the Mid-Atlantic region, within reach of large population centers. Though still little known, they are certain to become popular.

Virginia's highest mountain, Mount Rogers (5,279 feet), and its neighbor, Whitetop, for instance, are crowned by a northern-type forest of Fraser fir and red spruce, which make them a unique laboratory for scientists, educators and students of all ages. These two peaks are the focal point of Mount Rogers National Recreation Area, a part of Thomas Jefferson National Forest in the heart of the Blue Ridge Mountains of southwest Virginia.

Roads wind through the valleys and rise past alpine-like mountain meadows. Footpaths to the summits lead upward through a northern hardwood forest and past massive boulders, which are part of the rock formations underlying the slender cloth of vegetation. The mountain streams are known to fishermen for their native trout and the woodlands to hunters for their deer and small game. Development of the Recreation Area will be complemented by the new Mount Rogers State Park. Both are near Abingdon, once a frontier gateway into the wilds of Kentucky and Tennessee, and now the home of the famous Barter Theatre.

In the neighboring state of West Virginia, Spruce Knob-Seneca Rocks National Recreation Area offers some of the same, and different, outdoor experiences. White water canoeing is popular with experts on swift-flowing streams that form the headwaters of the Potomac River in this part of Monongahela National Forest. An especially favorite course starts at Mouth of Seneca and winds downstream through canyons for 15 miles. In addition, Seneca Rocks, at the Mouth of Seneca, is one of the highest, most impressive rock formations in the East. Rock climbers come from hundreds of miles away to test their skills. According to legend, Snow Bird, the daughter of a Seneca chieftain, held a contest here to choose the brave she would wed. The first warrior to scale the cliff (which she had been able to climb since childhood) won her hand, so the story goes.

*Right: Serene Spruce Knob Lake in the Monongahela National Forest is set amid the misty Allegheny Mountains and some of the East's most spectacular country.*

Spruce Knob, the highest point in West Virginia (4,860 feet), is bordered by many species of plant life found far south of their normal range. Roadside overlooks are numerous at high elevations, with beautiful vistas into valleys of both Virginia and West Virginia. A trail leads to the cool summit.

One hundred million people live within 500 miles of the parallel mountain ridges contained within the National Recreation Area. But its purpose is not only to provide recreation for today but to "preserve important resources for future generations." Accordingly, the quiet green character in the heart of the hills will be protected through cooperative regional planning to "promote a harmonious and unified development of the National Recreation Area and the surrounding region." This beautiful but economically depressed region may yet come into its own through the wise use of its rich recreational resources.

In a different mountain setting almost a continent away, water-based recreation affords the principal attraction at Whiskeytown-Shasta-Trinity National Recreation Area. It lies in northern California, within a day's drive of San Francisco, Sacramento and Portland, centered around Whiskeytown Dam, which President John F. Kennedy dedicated in 1963 as part of the Central Valley Reclamation Project. Two of the three units are in Shasta-Trinity National Forest.

*Sawtooth National Forest: Aerial view across southwest end of Big Redfish Lake, noted for two species of salmon, chinook and landlocked kokanee.*

*Sawtooth Wilderness Area, Idaho: Breaking camp after
a night spent on the shores of Lake Toxaway.*

The 29,000-acre Shasta Lake, with 365 miles of shoreline, forms the core of the Shasta Unit, north of Redding. In the Trinity Unit the 16,000 acres of Clare Engle Lake and Lewiston Lake offer an added 145 miles of shoreline. Both units furnish facilities for boating, water skiing, scuba diving and fishing, and for hiking, riding and hunting on surrounding lands. The Shasta-Trinity Alps Primitive Area, a short distance northwest of Clare Engle Lake, complements the water-based recreation activities.

The Whiskeytown Unit, also highly popular, lies south of the National Forest and is administered by the National Park Service.

A region of natural beauty that is Idaho's pride, extending from cattle and sheep rangeland up through highland lakes and streams to 11,000-foot snowy pinnacles, has been awaiting Congressional approval as the newest National Recreation Area. An hour's drive north of Sun Valley, it embraces the Sawtooth Primitive Area, over 200,000 acres in the Sawtooth and Boise National Forests, where the Salmon River is born in snow crevices and cascading waterfalls. The Sawtooths are the home of deer, elk, mountain goat, bear and mountain lion, and were a special favorite of Gary Cooper and Ernest Hemingway.

The Sawtooths are popular today with hikers, climbers, trail riders and fishermen. In the valley, Redfish Lake, the largest lake, is noted for two species of salmon, the chinook and landlocked kokanee. The visitor center at the lakeshore interprets broad phases of natural and human history, including the lusty mining days of the late 19th century. Elsewhere in the proposed Recreation Area, remains of mining camps—Sawtooth City and Vienna—are being preserved to tell their story for themselves.

In the same region of the country, Flaming Gorge Dam, a graceful, slender concrete structure rising 502 feet above the Green River in eastern Utah, was designed primarily to produce hydroelectric power. But since completion in 1962 the 91-mile-long lake behind it has proven ideal for boating, fishing, swimming, and the surrounding land of the proposed Flaming Gorge National Recreation Area ideal for hiking, camping, hunting and nature study.

79

*Craggy rocks and tall evergreens*
*create a rugged setting*
*for this tumbling forest stream.*

*Starfish at low tide on beach at Cape Perpetua, in Oregon's Siuslaw National Forest.*

*Exploring along Oneonta Creek, Mt. Hood National Forest, where it flows between basaltic walls.*

*The Sylvania Recreation Area in Michigan's Upper Peninsula is a vignette of virgin northwoods.*

From the visitor center on the cliff edge overlooking the rainbow colored strata in Red Canyon, one can see how the twisting gorge is actually a slash in the flank of the mighty High Uintas, formed by renewed lifting, bending and folding over the centuries and by the cutting action of the Green River; and one can learn of the adventures of men like John Wesley Powell, who named the Flaming Gorge during his classic river exploration of 1869. The incredible plants and wildflowers on display are real, their blossoms carefully preserved by using sand from the shores of the Great Salt Lake.

Such visitor centers deal with many facets of land and people. Some have come into being through strange circumstances. For example, atop an earth and rock dam formed naturally in August 1959, when an earthquake sent the whole face of a mountain cascading across Madison River and up the opposite side, stands the Madison River Earthquake Area Visitor Center.

*Below: The 1959 Montana earthquake caused the face of this mountain to cascade across the Madison River and up the opposite side (foreground).*

It is near West Yellowstone, Montana, in the Gallatin National Forest. Exhibits explain what happened that fateful day when 80 million tons of rock raced at a speed of 100 miles an hour and buried some 20 campers, and tell the historic story of earthquakes.

Madison River is one of three visitor centers in Montana. Man's struggle against wildfire, and improvements since the early 1900's, when firefighters had only picks, shovels and axes, are depicted at the Missoula Visitor Center. Exhibits show the activities of the Equipment Development Center, Northern Forest Fire Laboratory and the famous Smokejumpers, all of which are headquartered here. Guided tours are conducted through the Smokejumpers' three-story parachute loft.

The third visitor center in Montana, Hungry Horse, is almost due north of Missoula, in a forested canyon near Kalispell. It affords a view of the face of Hungry Horse Dam and the lake formed behind it on the south fork of the Flathead River. The center interprets the story of water, accumulating as rain or snow on the high slopes of Flathead National Forest and flowing into the Columbia River and outward to the Pacific Ocean. It also tells of the resources of the Flathead National Forest, which covers 2,300,000 acres, much of it in commercial timber, and much in the Bob Marshall Wilderness and Mission Mountains Primitive Area.

In the Southwest, archaeology and human history are the themes at the Gila Cliff Dwelling Visitor Center, 43 miles from Silver City, New Mexico, operated jointly by the staffs of Gila National Monument and Gila National Forest. The dwellings are small, but interesting and well preserved in the face of an overhanging cliff chosen by the earliest Americans as their refuge in this remote corner of the Southwest. The center also shows how the hazy mountains were penetrated by white men during the silver, gold and grazing boom of the late 19th century.

Also in the arid lands, Sabino Canyon Visitor Center tells the story of life communities in the Southwest. It lies at the foot of the Santa Catalina Mountains and the start of the Hitchcock Highway, which leads upward to Mount Lemmon, outside of Tucson, Arizona, in Coronado National Forest. Here the visitor can learn to identify the varied plants of the desert, from short-lived wildflowers to the towering saguaro cactus. The magic time on the two self-guiding nature trails is spring, when the desert flowers are in bloom.

On a rocky headland where the forest meets the sea, the Cape Perpetua Visitor Center, a unit of the Siuslaw National Forest, introduces the traveler to a living natural museum of another kind—the Oregon Coast. Nature trails lead to shell mounds, left by ancient coastal Indians, and to tidal pools glistening from a profusion of growing things, including sea urchins, flowerlike anemones, hermit crabs, starfish and kelp swaying in the waves. The Trail of the Whispering Spruce affords one of Oregon's most spectacular views, 800 feet above the sea.

Mark Twain, in his Western newspaper days, apparently failed to describe the Oregon Coast, but he did cross a crest in the Sierras from Virginia City, Nevada, where he worked, to look down at Lake Tahoe. "A noble sheet of blue water," he observed, "the fairest picture the whole earth affords." The setting around the lake has changed much, and the qualities of the lake are endangered by pollution, but the green forests of the Sierra Nevada Mountains above it are protected in Eldorado National Forest, and interpreted at the Lake Tahoe Visitor Center near Camp Richardson.

Far to the North, the face of Mendenhall Glacier, a mile and a half wide and up to 200 feet high, located in the Tongass National Forest, outside Juneau, Alaska, can be viewed from the impressive Mendenhall Glacier Visitor Center, built into an outcrop of bedrock scoured and polished by recent glacial action. Telescopes are provided to help spot mountain goats on the cliffs above the glacier, which is a small portion of the vast Juneau Ice Field. This visitor center is one of the most popular places in Alaska with summer tourists; it is also jammed in winter for weekly lecture programs explaining glaciation.

A unique natural area where orchids and cranberries grow in mountain bogs—similar to vegetation in the low areas of Maine—is the subject of the Cranberry Mountain Visitor Center near Richwood, West Virginia, in the Monongahela National Forest. Two miles west of the center a self-guiding boardwalk trail leads across a small portion of the famous Cranberry Glades and introduces the visitor to plants, birds and mammals of the northern tundra. The soil is mainly sphagnum and sedge peat up to 11 feet deep underlain with algal ooze and clay. Carnivorous sundew and horned bladderwort, rare in the southern Alleghenies, are highly esteemed.

Further south, the Cradle of Forestry Visitor Center, 20 miles from Asheville, North Carolina, in the Pisgah National Forest, commemorates the site where forestry was first practiced and taught in the United States. The story begins with one of the world's wealthiest men, George Washington Vanderbilt, who arrived in this western section of North Carolina after considering many locations at which to build a great country home. To lay out his estate, which he called Biltmore, Vanderbilt engaged Frederick Law Olmstead, then at the peak of his career in landscape architecture. Though most associated with the design of public parks and university grounds, it was Olmstead who recommended that forest management be instituted here. To develop the practical plan, he advised Vanderbilt to engage young Gifford Pinchot, lately returned from his study of forestry in Europe.

*Left: The endless variety of forms of the saguaro cactus can be seen by visitors to several National Forests.*

Pinchot arrived in 1891. Initially, he found, the estate covered about 7,000 acres. Then Vanderbilt purchased other land in the mountains, which he called Pisgah Forest, blessed with no less than 70 kinds of trees. In 1892 practical forestry began, with improvement cuttings, harvesting of old and unsound trees, and protecting the area from fire. Three years later Pinchot left for other fields and was succeeded by a prominent German forester, Carl Alwin Schenck. Many future leaders of his profession were trained by Schenck at the Biltmore Forest School, which he operated from 1898 to 1913 in a beautiful section called the Pink Beds (named for the pinkish color of kalmia, or mountain laurel). Today a trail leads from the visitor center to restored school rooms, dormitory and typical Black Forest lodge of the sort that Vanderbilt located around his large estate.

On the highest mountain in Georgia (4,784 feet), the Brasstown Bald Visitor Center, a unit of the Chattahoochee National Forest, overlooks the rugged mountains of southern Appalachia, with portions of four states visible from the observation deck. The uniquely designed center is one of the finest vantage points for fall color viewing. Displays recount the history of the Cherokee Indians, who hunted the abundant game and found safety in the hills until gold was discovered in the 1820's and they were forced to migrate to the West over the infamous Trail of Tears.

In another part of the South, Blanchard Springs Cavern, near Mountain View, Arkansas, in the Ozark National Forest, typifies the unusual features still being discovered, developed and interpreted. Although it is one of the most beautiful caverns in the nation, Blanchard's scientific and recreation values were not fully realized until a study of recent years made by the Forest Service with the cooperation of speleological groups. A project to construct trails and an elevator entrance has been underway since 1966. The first tours will be conducted in 1970. And a new visitor center will interpret the forest of stalagmites and stalactites under the Ozarks.

*Salmon National Forest: Welcome, Harbor and Wilson Lakes in the Big Horn Crags area.*

Many kinds of migrations have crossed the National Forests. After the two intrepid French traders, Radisson and Groseilliers, discovered beaver in northern Minnesota, the French established their fur-trading route linking the western waters with Montreal. Their adventures in the wild and beautiful country are depicted at the Voyageur Visitor Center, at Ely, portal to Superior National Forest, even including a handcrafted *voyageur* cargo canoe. Dioramas show how lakes were carved by glaciers in the ice age and how Indians were as much a part of the forest as trees, water and wildlife. For the benefit of visitors heading into the Boundary Waters Canoe Area, a canoe-handling demonstration is given on the grounds.

About 120 miles to the southeast of Superior National Forest, across Lake Superior at the western end of Michigan's Upper Peninsula, lies the Sylvania Recreation Area.

"Sylvania is unique. There is no area like it, nor will there be, giving in one compact area a vignette of virgin northwoods and pristine lakes."

With these words, the Forest Service has endeavored to describe the quality involved in one of the most important additions to public ownership in the Midwest (or anywhere in America) in many years.

The Sylvania tract, near Watersmeet and just a few miles from the Wisconsin border, was acquired in 1967 through the Land and Water Conservation Fund as part of Ottawa National Forest. Its 18,000 acres, previously used as an exclusive hunting preserve with minimum development and very little cutting, have become the core of this 54,000-acre recreation area.

"The stately trees, some forest giants, sway with the cool winds that sweep across the Upper Peninsula," continues the description. "There are interesting mixtures of sugar maple, yellow birch, Eastern hemlock, oaks, aspen, and scattered red and white pine monarchs. Trees are of all ages from veterans to seedlings. In these stands you can see the panorama of ecological interactions and development clearly depicted."

The administration of Sylvania represents an unusual challenge to safeguard and accent the truly qualitative experience the public deserves, by protecting the ecological life communities of the area's bog, muskeg and forest, and limiting human use. "Overdevelopment must be avoided," the Forest Service warned before the area was acquired. "The intensity and kind of recreation use cannot be allowed to destroy the beauty and charm of Sylvania that make it so desirable."

Many developed—and lightly used—recreation areas are available on nearby scenic lakes within the National Forest, with clear water, boat-launching sites and good swimming. This explains why the Forest Service allows parking only on the periphery of Sylvania and reserves the old primitive roads for use as walking trails, and why motors are not permitted on a large number of lakes—one of which is called Glimmerglass and another, as though summing up the qualitative essence of Sylvania, Golden Silence.

*Horsemen on the trail near Cathedral Peak in the picturesque Salmon National Forest.*

# VI | Rendezvous with the Land

In the chaos of depression America, almost two million men and women abandoned all pretense to a permanent home life. They took to the roads and the rails, traveling on foot or in freight cars, sleeping wherever night overcame them, in caves, shanty towns and flophouses, adrift from society, floating with the aimless tides of the time. Among them were a quarter of a million young people, the "teenage tramps of America," wandering the land in company with their lost destiny.

The drifters were only a fraction of the total of jobless youth. Most were left in their home environments, tramping city streets or stagnating in country towns. In 1932, about one-fourth of all young people between the ages of 15 and 24 in the labor market were unemployed, while another one-fourth worked only part time.

The new administration of Franklin D. Roosevelt in 1933 had to cope with the fate of these young people. It also faced deep national scars of a very different kind. Through generations of waste and misuse, much of the nation's treasure in timber resources had been destroyed. The consequence of planless abuse of the forests and fields was erosion, accounting for three billion tons of soil washing downstream each year. A like amount was blown away by wind. Deserts of dust continually replaced the grasslands of the plains.

Throughout the election campaign of 1932 Roosevelt had conducted correspondence with Gifford Pinchot, then the Republican governor of Pennsylvania, and other conservation leaders, gathering their views on a program to combat soil erosion and timber famine through self-sustaining public work. In mid-November, following the election, the Secretary of Agriculture-designate, Henry A. Wallace, and Roosevelt's economic adviser, Rexford Guy Tugwell, asked the Chief of the Forest Service, Robert Y. Stuart, if he could develop plans to put 25,000 men to work in the National Forests.

Such relief work had already begun on a limited scale. In California and Washington, the Forest Service had cooperated with state and county officials in running subsistence camps for the unemployed. Local authorities had clothed and fed the men, while the Forest Service had sheltered them and directed their work. Accordingly, Stuart responded with certainty that the Forest Service could handle 25,000 men usefully—but within a month he was advised further that the anticipated number would be increased ten fold!

Thus the Civilian Conservation Corps, the CCC, was born. It was a part of the American scene for nine years, until 1942, and part of the lives of 2,500,000 young Americans who passed through its ranks.

CCC became the most highly regarded and popular New Deal agency, championed by Republicans as well as Democrats. At its high point, between 1935 and 1937, there were 1,500 camps with a peak enrollment of 500,000. That period was still a low point of the depression and most men came in the final act of despair and helplessness. They enlisted in what was primarily a work program, but found a healthy return to the land, the making of many of them. CCC also enrolled technical assistants to furnish leadership, including men who later became leaders in land conservation agencies.

The first crude camps were tent cities; in time they evolved into more sophisticated barracks in the backwoods. These were the outposts of "Roosevelt's Tree Army." Of all the forest planting in the history of the nation, more than half was done by CCC. A large majority of the camps worked on projects administered by the Department of Agriculture, and most of them were in national, state or private forests, under direction of the Forest Service.

The boys had to work and work hard, toiling with their hands. In retrospect, the sum total of their common achievement was epochal, in many ways they turned the tide in promoting the salvation of America's natural resources.

During the CCC era the acreage lost by fire reached its lowest point ever, even though a record number of fires were reported, in which 47 enrollees gave their lives. CCC's unique contribution was its ability to mobilize a readily available, large, trained fire-fighting force. In one case, 1,400 men were dispatched to a fire near Los Angeles with such speed that a potential disaster was controlled before damaging either the National Forest or nearby urban area. CCC boys opened thousands of miles of fire breaks, over 60,000 miles of trail; they built 600 lookout towers, scores of water storage basins and well digging units to assure a ready supply of water for tanks and pumps.

*Right: Dust storms, one result of long abuse of the land, helped to bring about the need for CCC in 1930's.*

*CCC workers in Pisgah National Forest in 1937: Young men such as these built campgrounds and restored historic sites.*

In other forestry activities, they built roads and trails, opening large areas to timber use for the first time. They thinned overcrowded timber stands, managed experimental plots, fought bark beetles, gypsy moths, white pine blister rust and other infestations and diseases. They improved grazing lands of the western National Forests by re-seeding thousands of acres, digging water holes, building fences and bridges.

CCC was an immense force in the field of recreation. Many facilities developed in the thirties are still in use a generation later, and may continue to be used generations hence. The National Park Service, which had the largest number of camps in the Department of Interior, successfully utilized the corps to develop entire new parks, including the mighty Big Bend National Park in Texas. CCC boys built bridges, picnic and campgrounds, constructed roads and trails; they restored La Purisima Mission in California, now one of the finest state historic parks, and reconstructed Fort Necessity in Pennsylvania, the scene of George Washington's first test in the French and Indian War. They built hundreds of campgrounds in National Parks and National Forests. They served other agencies, including the Bureau of Reclamation, Soil Conservation Service, and Bureau of Biological Survey, now the Fish and Wildlife Service. In the famous "Arkansas float camp," enrollees working for the latter agency lived on a fleet of houseboats while developing waterfowl refuges in streams, swamps and bayous, and were given "shore leave" on weekends.

*Savage flames destroy valuable trees in the Brushy Creek fire of 1961 in the Salmon National Forest, Idaho.*

The financial return of CCC, its long range value to the nation, is impossible to determine. There is no way of calculating how much was saved by the fire prevention or grazing programs, or the extent to which the planting of billions of trees and erosion control increased land values and helped to produce better crops and livestock.

CCC was subject to criticism, like any program of its kind. The Army controlled, and perhaps overcontrolled, the camps. The Negro American did not gain his proper share of the program, and never took part without discrimination. Education was one of the less successful endeavors. Sometimes the "development" in natural areas resulted in overdevelopment.

For many young Americans, however, CCC proved the turning point of their lives. It was their first chance at fresh air, good food, and a feeling that someone in the world cared about them. Illiterates were taught to read and write. Many obtained high school diplomas. Forty universities gave courses to CCC camps by mail. Some boys won academic scholarships, others won football scholarships through the athletic program, and a few went from CCC baseball fields to the big leagues.

The CCC, in short, was a big league in itself that brought light into the darkest corners of the nation. It was an experiment that brought youth into contact with the land to the benefit of both.

*Beyond the great panoramas, there is much to be seen in National Forests by those who will take the time to focus down.*

*Moldering tree stump, surrounded
by delicate ferns, is slowly being
covered over by moss.*

*Job Corpsmen in Pisgah National
Forest, North Carolina, carry on
in the tradition of CCC.*

*Work call line-up at CCC camp in Chippewa National Forest in 1940: CCC was an immense force in recreation and conservation.*

In 1964, almost 30 per cent of the two million young people entering the nation's work force were school dropouts. They were from the breeding grounds of dark, unhappy urban ghettoes or rural slums. Many had never worked for wages. There were jobs to be had but they had difficulty in finding work because they had no skills, and most were unable to hold a job whenever they found one.

In recognition of their dire plight, Congress declared a policy "to eliminate the paradox of poverty in the midst of plenty in this nation by opening to everyone the opportunity for education and training, the opportunity to work, and the opportunity to live in decency and dignity." It established a new force called the

*A birch tree in the Chippewa National Forest gracefully silhouetted against the autumn sky of Minnesota.*

Youth Conservation Corps, as part of the Job Corps, to be assigned to camps where work activity would be directed "toward conserving, developing and managing the public natural resources of the nation and developing, managing and protecting public recreation areas."

One year later, over 5,500 young men between the ages of 16 and 21 were enrolled in 50 centers, and by 1967 the numbers of men and camps both were doubled.

The largest conservation center in the country was located at Pine Knot, 30 miles south of Somerset, within the boundaries of Daniel Boone National Forest in the Appalachian hills of Kentucky. Its complement at a typical period included 166 Negro Americans, 60 whites, five Spanish-Americans, one Indian, and one Eskimo. They lived together, worked together, played together and on occasions had their misunderstandings, but this was part of the process of learning to live in a community.

*Typing class at Job Corps Conservation Center in Texas: Without training, many of these young men would end up on welfare rolls.*

Many were away from home for the first time, facing problems of new places and new faces. The first weeks were the hardest. One boy who came as a troublemaker refused to follow instructions and defied discipline until he realized that if he was sent home there would be nothing for him but to roam the streets and the blind alleys to nowhere. Then he straightened out. He was typical of many who had to work themselves up from a very low level. The challenge of the camp was to make them realize that they could, that there was a reason to, and to help them take the first step toward finding their potential and self-respect as useful citizens.

"Many of our boys have come from broken homes and without proper guidance could go astray," Dale O. Fisher, the director of the camp, said in a talk to a local Rotary Club. "Some are right on the fence when we get them.

"Without training, many undoubtedly would end up on the welfare rolls as non-productive citizens, and some would be criminals. Critics may say this is an expensive program. But it costs far less to train and educate a boy in Job Corps in the short run than to keep a person on relief or a prisoner in the penitentiary in the long run."

Pine Knot was chosen as the location of the camp because of its nearness to conservation projects and emerging new recreation areas, little known outside of the region but outstanding in their potential. Among these are Yahoo Falls, a beautiful 116-foot-high waterfall; Natural Arch, a massive sandstone arch, reached by footpath in the forest; and Beaver Creek Wildlife Management Area, setting of the first successful effort to restore deer and turkey to the woods of eastern Kentucky. Likewise, the Frenchburg Job Corps Camp in the northern part of the National Forest was near other woodland and wildlife trails and Natural Bridge State Park.

These were two of 47 camps on various National Forests throughout the country, conducted by the Forest Service in cooperation with the Office of Economic Opportunity. There were as many more located in National Parks and Monuments, Wildlife Refuges, Bureau of Reclamation Projects, Bureau of Land Management areas, and state lands. These Conservation Centers were part of the overall Job Corps program, which also included Urban Centers.

When the boys arrived at Pine Knot they found a modern facility set in a world of trees and cool clean air. The faculty and staff lived in a park of mobile homes, while all the rest of the buildings were uniform in appearance—built of wood, reddish brown in color, and unmistakably new.

On arrival they received uniforms and equipment. Some became owners of toothbrushes for the first time in their lives and then had to be shown how to use them, and they were given other basic lessons in personal hygiene and sanitation. They were evaluated for reading ability and placed in three separate categories. Over a span of the first year almost 40 per cent were classified as "pre-readers," who could neither read nor write. Another 40 per cent were "intermediates," with reading ability between third and sixth grades, and the remainder were "advanced," with reading skills of seventh grade or higher.

The corpsmen were assigned to an education program divided in two parts and geared to their individual learning abilities. The first part involved the most elemental education. The reading program, for instance, was designed to enable them to use a library and to read the average book, magazine, newspaper and vocational training material. The minimum goal was to have trainees reading at somewhere between seventh and eighth grade levels, if not higher. Mathematics was another basic course (some boys at the outset could barely count to ten), involving training in addition, subtraction, multiplication and division. Other classes were devoted to proper work attitudes and habits—promptness, neatness, how to conduct a telephone conversation and to work as a member of a team—the kinds of things that would make them valuable to future employers in their chosen jobs. Corpsmen classified as "advanced" students were encouraged to study at a more rapid pace in a program for high school equivalency operated by the University of Kentucky. It was a banner day at Pine Knot in October 1966, when Gene Colbert, of Culpeper, Virginia, became the first corpsman to complete his examination and receive his diploma.

*Job Corpsmen working on trail in Ouachita National Forest, Arkansas: There were 47 Corps Camps in National Forests in 1967.*

The second part of the education program was vocational, teaching skills in welding and auto mechanics. The welding students learned classroom theory and had enough practical shopwork in using a torch to qualify as first class welder's helpers. The auto mechanics learned to take cars apart and put them together. Frenchburg, the other Job Corps camp in the National Forest, specialized in mechanics, cooking, offset printing and power saw operation.

A few who showed interest and aptitude in heavy equipment work were transferred to the Jacobs Creek Job Corps Conservation Center near Bristol, Tennessee, in the Cherokee National Forest, the only one of its kind in the country. There, through a cooperative effort of the International Union of Operating Engineers and the Forest Service, selected corpsmen were trained in operation and maintenance of heavy equipment such as scrapers, bulldozers and road graders. Besides classwork and shop work, they had on-the-job-training, building recreation access roads in the National Forest. Of 79 starting the first class in November 1966, 52 completed the twelve-month course successfully. The union then helped to find them jobs in 20 states at starting wages appreciably above the national average for their age group—that is, all but two who were kept on to help in training the second class.

Pine Knot, the little city in the hills, was no vacation spot. "We do not try to turn out angels here," said Joe Ferguson, the education director, "but rather self-sufficient individuals." Some corpsmen couldn't take the routine, or didn't like it, and quit. Some who stuck

*Job Corps Center in San Juan National Forest in Colorado:*
*Part of the education program is geared toward elemental education.*

it out went on to college; one received a scholarship at nearby Somerset Community College. A few became Job Corps recruiters, feeling that they owed a debt for their training.

The Pine Knot day began at 6 a.m. with reveille and physical education. The boys ate three hot meals a day in the huge mess hall, with the sign at the serving line proclaiming, "This is the best mess in Job Corps!" After classes and work projects were done, they had time to relax in the gymnasium with basketball, boxing and other indoor sports, and in the recreation center, where a few learned wood carving and other handicrafts instead of playing pool.

A local community advisory board was established in Pine Knot to aid in developing harmonious relations between the community and the camp. Small towns fearfully anticipated disturbances from Job Corpsmen and on that ground often spurned offers to have camps located nearby. Problems, however, arose only on rare occasions. The Kentucky camps were more of an asset than Kentuckians anticipated. On one occasion the Pine Knot Corpsman Council raised $180 in donations and then purchased Christmas packages for local needy families. Four corpsmen made a private project of cleaning shelves and rearranging books at the Winchester Library. "Thanks, Job Corps," said an editorial in the Clay City Times in March 1967, after 14 boys had shifted rolls of newsprint about to be damaged by a late winter flood.

The conservation work performed by each man was less than in the CCC, because the Job Corps devoted more time to education. The achievements were still considerable in Kentucky and wherever the corps operated. By the end of 1967 the corpsmen had constructed 10,000 new camping and picnic units; improved more than 16,000 acres of wildlife habitat; planted 16,000 acres of trees and shrubs, and improved or reforested 13,000 acres of timberlands.

In the West, Operation Rehab in 1965 saw 200 corpsmen in California and Oregon cleaning up and repairing areas devastated by Christmas floods. It set a pattern in which corpsmen were repeatedly involved as shock troops in helping troubled areas. And in some forested and rural sections the Job Corps represented the sole source of available firefighting crews.

For the boys of the Job Corps, like those of the CCC, their experience was a rendezvous with the land and with their own destiny. They learned, often for the first time, the pride in doing a job well, and the pride of belonging and being wanted.

For the nation these projects furnished a rendezvous, too. It met its responsibility in conserving, rather than wasting, the most valuable and crucial resource of all, the human resource.

*Right: Corpsman constructing fireplace grate for camping area as part of vocational aspect of education program.*

# VII | Scenic Rivers

The rivers shaped the land. When man arrived the rivers became avenues of destiny, first to the birchbark canoe, then to the raft, flatboat and barge. In the advance of history the rivers were clogged with logs, and afloat with pioneers, traders and warriors, while their banks became lined with cities and industries. Always there seemed more streams untapped, waiting for a young Huck Finn or Tom Sawyer to get his small share of natural heritage close to home.

It is said that some three million miles of river channel flow across the face of the United States. Today almost all of this vast watery network has been harnessed to serve the material needs of people. The St. Lawrence links inland America with shipping channels of the world. The Ohio carries the works of industry on its surface. The Mississippi joins commercial centers of the North with its outlet to the sea below New Orleans. The Columbia, that once brought Lewis and Clark to the conquest of their empire, provides light and hydro-electric power to the Northwest.

We need harnessed and developed rivers. But we need other kinds of rivers, too. The nation has under-taken over the years to protect parks and forests, to establish refuges for wildlife and reservoirs to conserve water. But most of the rivers, though woven into the romance, literature and soul of the surrounding land, have been sacrificed to progress. Only a small number of streams remain untamed, unspoiled, approaching the natural conditions in which man found them. Now Congress has considered legislation to establish a National Scenic Rivers System. The concept of this system recognizes the need of pleasant scenic rivers close to big cities, that can be viewed by car; semi-wild, and wild rivers that must be reached by footpath or horse trail and are removed from the smells and sounds of mechanized civilization. We need them all, in balance, to assure survival of a society that is truly civilized.

Many of the rivers under review as possible candidates for the National Scenic Rivers System are in the National Forests. They are special places to visit and enjoy, where young men test their hardiness by running the rapids and older men can find their contact with nature in a float trip and camp-out on a gravel bar, where artists of all ages can find inspirational source matter, and where natural scientists, whether of the Boy Scout or professional variety, can pursue the miracles of life.

These free-flowing rivers survive with natural shore-line borders of trees, bluffs or open meadows. They are really for all people, preserving a quality of the true America that future generations deserve to know.

The nation requires clear water for the enjoyment of its scenic rivers, and for many other uses as well. One hardly thinks of the National Forests as a "water factory," considering that the major thrust of past years has been to heal gullies, establish a cover of vegetation on bare soil, and to minimize erosion through diverse techniques. But watershed specialists *can* deliver substantial amounts of water previously lost through evaporation to streams, irrigation ditches, reservoirs and water mains—water that does not reach these places now.

High elevation areas of the National Forests are the accumulation centers of heavy snow and rain. Through careful resource management practices, the potential increase in surface runoff is estimated at between 10 and 15 per cent, which could mean up to 15 million acre-feet of new water per year. For those who think in terms of dish pans and bath tubs, this volume is the equivalent of about four trillion gallons, enough to supply the domestic needs of the entire population for over a year; it would also prove adequate to produce 25 million tons of food and fibre through irrigation.

Many methods are being employed to produce this "new water." Timber harvesting can be designed to produce deep accumulation of snow between uncut portions of the forest stand. In this manner snow melts more slowly, produces water later in the summer, and loses less moisture to the air through evaporation. In appropriate areas, snow fences are placed to encourage long lasting drifts. Artificial avalanching can also be used to build deep snow deposits with delayed runoff. In other areas, selective removal of streamside plants which use large quantities of water and conversion to less thirsty types is common.

All these techniques, of course, need to be practiced with careful attention to aesthetic, recreation, soil, wilderness, fish and wildlife values. Water production is not the sole objective in itself, but rather one component of a complex mixture of goals. At their best, these improvement measures reduce the threat of floods in spring and provide a steady flow of water in place of drought. They also mean that fewer canoes and rafts will break up or strike high center on rocks and bars maneuvering down the scenic rivers.

One of the finest and wildest rivers of them all is the Rogue in southern Oregon. The Rogue River Recreation Area covers about 25,000 acres in the heart of forested mountains, with a 36-mile stretch of deep green water, proud with natural power, that alternately races through rapids, glides softly and gracefully, then churns into foam between great boulders. "The happiest lot of any angler would be to live somewhere along the banks of the Rogue River," Zane Grey once wrote, "the most beautiful stream of Oregon, and the coldest, swiftest, deepest stream I ever fished."

*Left: Grand Canyon of the Snake River, one of the deepest gorges in North America, lies astride the border of Idaho and Oregon.*

*Another view of the Snake River: Upper Mesa Falls on Henrys Fork has a drop of 105 feet.*

*Humboldt National Forest, Nevada: Lehman Creek as it flows through a grove of aspen in Wheeler Peak Scenic Area.*

Grey staked a mining claim while collecting facts and fiction for "Rogue River Feud." He recognized it for what it now remains—part of the last real West. It is joined by clear streams given such names by the early rivermen as Flea Creek, Painted Rock Creek, Lonetree Creek and Silver Creek. Those men were miners. Some carried out a fortune; others left stone pilings and mining ditches as their memorials.

The visitor who runs the river today does so over rocky riffles and looks up to towering canyon walls. If he's a fisherman he will have his mind on steelhead trout in the slicks above and below the riffles, but his eyes will not fail to scan scores of species of Western trees and plants constantly changing with soil, slope and drainage, staging a tremendous show of form and color. His companions will be birds ranging from water ouzels, sandpipers and killdeer up through tuneful canyon wren, kingfisher and cliff swallows, to vulture, hawks, osprey and blue heron, plus occasional deer and black bears (who are the best fishermen on the Rogue).

Lower Rogue River Recreation Area is part of the Siskiyou National Forest and is joined on the east by an additional 20 miles of rugged river and canyon administered by the Bureau of Land Management. Transportation is furnished by skillful boatmen, expert in the ways of the river world. Part of the area can also be covered on foot over the Rogue River Trail, first blazed in the wilderness by gold prospectors in the 1880's.

*Greer Spring in Mark Twain National Forest helps to make
Eleven Point River a remarkably clear stream.*

*An abundance of plants beside and on the water
at Alexander Springs, Ocala National Forest.*

*South branch of the Potomac River
flows past Eagle Rock in Monongahela
National Forest, West Virginia.*

*Aerial view of famous Boundary Waters Canoe Area shows Basswood, Crooked and Iron Lakes.*

*This clear-flowing stream at Juniper Springs is typical of Ocala National Forest.*

The Rogue is born in Crater Lake National Park. It flows westward past Grants Pass. The truly wild portion begins several miles beyond at Grave Creek and ends at Flea Creek. Then it continues, a little tamer, past the settlement of Agness, before splashing across the sands at Gold Beach and giving its water to the Pacific. Jet-powered boats carry passengers on the round trip from Gold Beach to Agness—affording a great many people an exciting run and a brief taste of the river. Enroute the boat passes several miles of forest recently acquired by the Forest Service through an exchange of lands with a timber company, a part of the program to safeguard the shoreline for public enjoyment.

For 130 miles from North Fork in Riggins, deep in the mountains of northern Idaho, the main Salmon River runs the gamut from tranquility to turbulence but is never twice the same. It passes traces of old mines, hot springs, homesteads and dude camps, and then flows between granite-walled canyons. The entire Salmon is a marvelous stream, without a dam to block its course from its headwaters in the Sawtooth Mountains to its confluence with the Snake. Eighty miles of the 130-mile reach are almost roadless and this is the famous stretch that gives the Salmon its name, "River of No Return." For more than 150 years after the first white man came into this country, only one-way trips were possible down this reach of the river, which flows through or forms the boundary between four National Forests—the Salmon, Payette, Bitterroot and Nezperce.

The road along the river from North Fork ends at a boat landing and Corn Creek campground. Beyond this point motor vehicles are prohibited. Many sportsmen shoot the wild river in kayaks. But the best way to travel for wildlife observation is in a float boat—a rubber raft. Along the rocks on shore one is not unlikely to spot mountain goat and sheep, or deer and elk, especially in spring; in dry, hot summers most animals go higher. Over the rough rapids called Devil's Teeth there may be a golden eagle soaring aloft, scanning the scene for his dinner. For many miles a boating party is alone with the river, shooting the rapids and watching the early run of Chinook salmon struggle to spawning grounds upstream. Float boaters can heave to on gravel or sand bars for the night and hear the *yip-yip* of the coyote.

*Kaibab National Forest, Arizona: The Colorado, one of the nation's great rivers, seen from Navajo Bridge.*

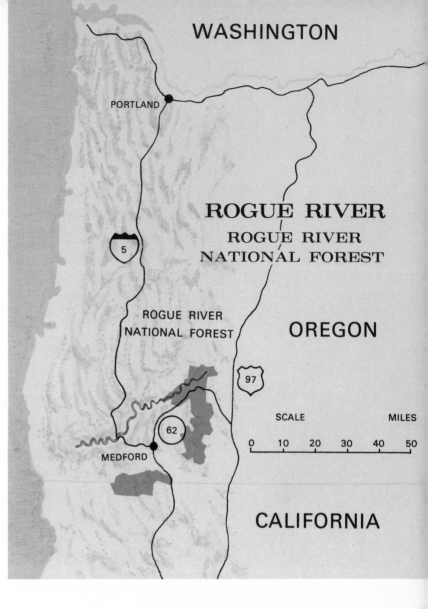

*Left: In June dogwood blooms along Oregon's Rogue River, one of the finest wild rivers in the United States.*

Campers can also use the simple facilities at Lantz Bar, named for Frank Lantz, a heroic figure of the main Salmon. As a firefighter trapped in the big blaze of 1929, his shoes were burned off; Lantz wrapped his shirt and pants on his feet and survived under the smoke by staying close to the waters of Sable Creek. A private outfitter once offered Lantz $20,000 for his land, but this mountain man preferred to sell to the Forest Service for $5,000 with rights of life tenancy—and he still greets visitors on the scene.

Four outfitters' tent camps are along the banks, popular with fishermen and hunters. In spring and fall power boats spot fishermen after steelhead and cutthroat trout along the way.

At Hancock Bar and Corn Creek Bar ancient Indian campsites are reminders that the earliest inhabitants came into Salmon River Canyon more than 5,000 years ago. An Army captain, after tracking the Sheep Eater Indians through these steep slopes in 1879, reported, "We have traveled over much of the country that no white man ever saw before, our guides and miners declaring we could not get through at all."

Hells Canyon, or the Grand Canyon of the Snake River, lies astride the border of Idaho and Oregon, near the confluence of the Salmon and Snake Rivers and largely within National Forest boundaries. It is one of the deepest gorges in North America, plunging 5,700 feet from one point of the canyon rim down to the river. It is wild, rugged country, one of the finest natural treasures of the Pacific Northwest.

Prior to the summer of 1967 Hells Canyon was due to be drowned by the proposed High Mountain Sheep Dam. A historic case then came before the United States Supreme Court, to determine whether the dam should be constructed by public or private power interests. The Court, however, questioned the wisdom of building any dam at all.

"The test," the Court declared, "is whether the project will be in the public interest, and that determination can be made only after an exploration of all issues relevant to the public interest." These issues, noted Justice William O. Douglas, include: future power demands and supply, future alternate sources of power, and "the public interest in preserving reaches of wild rivers and wilderness areas, the preservation of anadromous fish for commercial and recreational purposes, and the protection of wildlife." Thus, this free-flowing stretch of the beautiful river may not have been lost, after all.

*Rio Grande National Forest: The South Fork of the Rio Grande River in southwest-central Colorado.*

Rivers are the living arteries of the Ozarks, about 20 streams spring-born and spring-fed. Some have been dammed to form lakes of tremendous size—arenas for motorboating, water skiing, bass fishing and resort camping. To some, however, true Ozarkiana is still to be found in a float trip down a clear, swift-running stream like the Gasconade, Saint Frances, Black or Meremec, whose headwaters are cradled in Clark National Forest; in the Current River, which flows through the new Ozark National Scenic Riverway, administered by the National Park Service; or in the Eleven Point, which bends and winds between steep hollows and towering bluffs of the Mark Twain National Forest.

The Eleven Point is a favorite in southern Missouri for float fishing and camping. Such travel is in the Ozark tradition, recalling the days when each farm had a landing with a skiff or two (known as a flatboat, Long John, or just plain johnboat) tied to a handy tree root and when it was easier to get around on the back streams than on the back roads.

Many who float the river start at Greer Crossing, floating down through rushing rapids and alternating deep tranquil pools, passing Turners Mill, the last vestige of an old settlement called Surprise. The roads of today normally follow the ridgetops rather than the stream valleys, so that canoers can insulate themselves from everyday pursuits and thoughts. The Eleven Point is managed as a part of the National Forest to perpetuate this atmosphere. Along its course the river borders the wildest and least accessible area in the Eleven Point area called the Irish Wilderness. It was settled by a hardy band of Irishmen, but they were dispersed by bushwackers in the Civil War.

Rivers with sections in National Forests, which have received preliminary or detailed attention as part of the Interdepartmental Scenic Rivers Study:

| State | River | National Forest |
|---|---|---|
| Arizona | Colorado | Kaibab |
| | Salt | Tonto |
| Arkansas | Buffalo | Ozark |
| California | Feather (Middle Fork) | Plumas |
| | Kern (North Fork) | Sequoia |
| | Klamath | Klamath, Six Rivers |
| | Smith | Six Rivers, Siskiyou |
| Colorado | Animas | San Juan |
| | Cache la Poudre | Roosevelt |
| | White (North, South Forks) | White River |
| Florida | Oklawaha | Ocala |
| Georgia | Headwaters of Savannah | Chattahoochee |
| Idaho | Clearwater (Middle Fork) | Clearwater, Nezperce |
| | St. Joe | St. Joe |
| | Salmon | Nezperce, Payette, Salmon, Boise, Challis, Bitterroot Targhee |
| | Snake (North Fork) | |
| Kentucky | Cumberland | Daniel Boone |
| Michigan | Pere Marquette | Manistee |
| Missouri | Gasconade | Clark |
| | Eleven Point | Mark Twain |
| Montana | Big Hole | Beaverhead |
| | Blackfoot | Helena |
| | Flathead (North, Middle, South Forks) | Flathead |
| | Madison | Gallatin |
| | Yellowstone | Gallatin |
| Nebraska | Niobrara | Nebraska |
| New Mexico | Gila | Gila |
| | Rio Grande | Carson |
| North Carolina | Linville | Pisgah |
| | Headwaters of Savannah | Nantahala |
| | French Broad | Pisgah, Nantahala |
| Oregon | Deschutes | Deschutes |
| | Rogue | Siskiyou |
| South Carolina | Headwaters of Savannah | Sumter |
| Virginia | James | Jefferson, George Washington |
| | Shenandoah | George Washington |
| Washington | Hoh | Olympic |
| | Methow | Okanogan |
| | Skagit | Mount Baker |
| West Virginia | Cheat | Monongahela |
| | Cacapon | George Washington |
| | Greenbrier | Monongahela |
| | Potomac | Monongahela |
| Wisconsin | Namekagon | Chequamegon |
| | St. Croix | Chequamegon |
| | Wolf | Nicolet |
| Wyoming | Green | Bridger |
| | Gros Ventre | Teton |
| | Yellowstone | Gallatin |

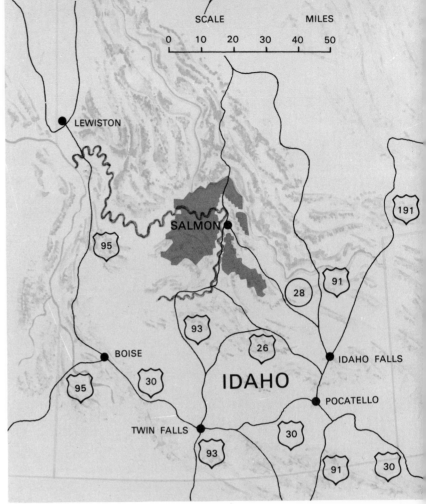

SALMON RIVER
SALMON RIVER NATIONAL FOREST

# VIII

# A New Age of Walking Americans

"Give me," says William Hazlitt, "the clear blue sky over my head, and the green turf beneath my feet, a winding road before me, and a three hours' march to dinner—then to thinking. It is hard if I cannot start some game on these lone heaths. I laugh, I run, I leap, I sing for joy."

There are many fine walks over the "lone heaths" and the high hills of the National Forests. They are for hikers, climbers, slow strollers and even for invalids; they are for everyone in every section of the country.

The trails in the National Forests are well used, for walking is one of those simple pleasures within economic reach of all citizens. Figures show that walking ranks among the most popular forms of outdoor recreation. Conditions of the times demand that it be so: A people whose everyday lives are circumscribed by mechanization and urbanization clamor for respite, a return to native ways. In order to survive and prosper as a race of thinking beings, we need to exercise our bodies in natural surroundings, for man is no synthetic creature, but a living offspring of the earth.

President Lyndon B. Johnson gave recognition to the New Age of Walking Americans in 1966 when he called for the establishment of many more trails for walking, hiking, horseback riding and cycling, both in rural areas and the back country. "Old and young alike can participate," he said. "Our doctors recommend and encourage such activity for fitness and fun."

Recreational trails have been the subject of proposed Federal legislation for many years, but as a result of the President's statement, a new concept was placed before Congress, providing for the establishment of a National System of Scenic Trails. The prime components of this system would be a number of choice trails with high natural, scenic or historic qualities, each one over several hundred miles in length, with overnight shelters at appropriate intervals, linked with other trails branching out to nearby points of special attraction. Such values would be safeguarded and enhanced for the benefit of generations to come.

The major arteries of three of the proposed National Scenic Trails run through the National Forest System, along the ridgelines, mountaintops, streams and lakeshores, harmonizing with the natural areas they cross, affording the visitor communion with the natural world and a feeling of true inspiration.

The genius of the long trails that now exist derives from the devotion of people who love the land. The Forest Service has been aided—and spurred—by the ideas, energy and unselfish activity of local outdoor clubs and individuals. Such groups have laid out, marked and maintained trails, cleaned the litter left by others, and encouraged wise use.

The Appalachian Trail has been envisioned as the foundation unit of the new national system. It is the longest marked path in the world, covering 2,021 miles along the crest of Appalachia from northern New England into the Deep South. It traverses 14 states. Virginia has the longest section, 500 miles; West Virginia, the shortest, 10 miles. The trail embraces 507 miles in eight National Forests (White Mountain, New Hampshire; Green Mountain, Vermont; George Washington and Jefferson, Virginia; Pisgah and Cherokee, North Carolina and Tennessee; Nantahala, North Carolina; and Chattahoochee, Georgia, where it reaches its southern terminus at Springer Mountain), as well as 172 miles through two National Parks, 452 miles through state lands and the remainder of the trail through private lands.

The "AT" is more than a footway; it is a concept of recreation brought to reality almost entirely through the voluntary efforts of patriotic people who felt the need to stir the pioneer spirit and to provide new generations of Americans with the lure of exploration. "This is to be a connected trail," declared the Constitution of the Appalachian Trail Conference, after its organizational meeting in 1925, "running as far as practicable over the summits of the mountains and through the wild lands of the Atlantic seaboard and adjoining states, from Maine to Georgia, to be supplemented by a system of primitive camps at proper intervals, so as to render accessible for tramping, camping, and other forms of primitive travel and living, the said mountains and wild lands, as a means of conserving and developing within this region, the primeval environment as a natural resource."

*Right: Back packing up Lappi Lake trail walk in the rugged Selway-Bitterroot Wilderness Area in western Montana.*

*The Appalachian Trail has been envisioned as the foundation unit of a proposed National Scenic Trails System.*

The idea of the Appalachian Trail was proposed in 1921 by the eminent Benton MacKaye, forester and regional planner. He formulated the project for the mountain footpath from his wanderings in his native New England forests. In 1922 the first part of the trail was constructed by hiking clubs of New York and New Jersey. New England had much to add with the trail systems of the Appalachian Mountain Club, Green Mountain Club and the Dartmouth Outing Club. In time other clubs were formed farther south. Now these non-professional enthusiasts cooperate in maintaining the route with Federal and state agencies.

The walker who sets out to cover the entire Appalachian Trail and averages 17 miles a day will complete his journey in 123 days and nights. He will be within 150 miles of half a dozen of the country's largest cities—Boston, New York, Philadelphia, Balti-more, Washington, Atlanta—and cross an occasional motorway, but essentially he would be far removed from the works of man. His lodgings would be campsites, shelters and cabins. He would know that what makes a mountain trail a supreme adventure is the combination of natural diversity, the touch of intimacy at hand, and the fullness of distant vistas. The AT has has all of these elements.

New Englanders have a long and vigorous tradition on the trails, dating from explorers like Henry David Thoreau and some of the oldest hiking clubs in the country. The Appalachian Mountain Club began cutting its first trails in 1876; its goals then, as now, were to "explore the mountains of New England and adjacent regions, and in general to cultivate an interest in geographical studies."

The AMC huts constitute the only system of its kind for the tramping vacationer who desires a degree of comfort, well cooked food and a bunk for the night at modest prices. The Madison Huts are near the highest hiking trail in the Northeast, within reach of the Great Gulf. Pinkham Notch, the largest hut (accommodating 100 in two buildings), lies just off a main road, but within minutes the hiker is enveloped in deep woods, then up the headwall of Tuckerman Ravine, a great glacial cirque enroute to the summit of Mount Washington.

The Forest Service and AMC have lived in close understanding for many years. When Gifford Pinchot developed the concept of modern conservation, and Theodore Roosevelt popularized it, the AMC was prepared to join in their campaign. It sponsored lectures by Pinchot, advocated the Weeks Bill to establish National Forests in the East and collaborated with other organizations of like convictions. Its efforts have benefited many people, through maintenance of hundreds of miles of hiking trails, construction of free trailside shelters, a wide program of education in canoeing, mountaineering and natural history, and in publication of guidebooks, maps and pamphlets.

The Long Trail, a "footpath in the wilderness," epitomizes the sort of camping and tramping that one might associate with the Green Mountains of Vermont. It is sophisticated in its simplicity, a search for exercise and for truths in nature, with few extraneous complications.

Conceived in 1909 by a schoolmaster, James P. Taylor, the Long Trail was blazed by a hardy band called the Green Mountain Club. Today its 1,500 members maintain the trail, which covers 255.3 miles, the full length of the state between the borders of Massachusetts and Canada, and a chain of 60 open shelters and cabins, spaced an average of 4.2 miles apart, where any comer is welcome.

For 80 miles in the southern section of the state, the Long Trail and Appalachian Trail advance as a National Scenic Trail through the Green Mountain National Forest, a gentle upland that in some sections reminds one of the Scottish hills with their spaths, lochs, moors and isolated villages. The beauty of this trail is sheer accessibility from numerous roads and side trails. One can walk an hour or all week. Tramping along an open summit, or in the deep woods, the scenery is monotony-free, always changing. An easy short trip starts near Mount Tabor Village in the southern district, passing ancient charcoal kilns, climbing an easy grade through a hardwood forest to Little Rock Pond, which reflects the timbered shoreline in its clear surface. Two shelters are located here, one on a small island reached by a bridge, the ideal spot for sequestered fishing and swimming.

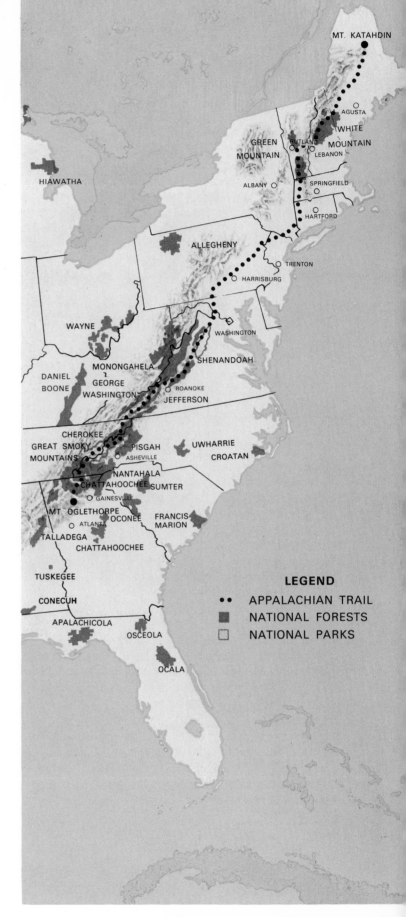

LEGEND
- • • APPALACHIAN TRAIL
- ▪ NATIONAL FORESTS
- □ NATIONAL PARKS

The proposed Continental Divide National Scenic Trail would provide a continuous route along the backbone of the Rocky Mountains for a distance of 3,082 miles from the Canadian border almost to the Mexican border, spanning spectacular, wild mountain country within view of great peaks over 14,000 feet, and rich in the early history of the West.

The concept of this trail was originated by a group of horsemen known as Rocky Mountain Trails, Inc. Later the Colorado Mountain Club joined in the effort. The two groups, in cooperation with the Forest Service, proceeded to establish the first segment between Empire and Rocky Mountain National Park in Colorado. Much remains to be done, including construction of 1,500 miles of new trail and the upgrading of another 1,100 miles.

This trail would pass through 23 National Forests and four National Parks, most of which have well developed trail systems. These trails and improved roads would provide access at many points along the way. Numerous old mining towns, like Bannock, Montana's first capital, and Leadville, Colorado, lie nearby. Throughout much of its length, however, the Continental Divide would be uncrossed by roads and remain remote from population centers.

In the Far West, the proposed Pacific Crest National Scenic Trail already is in existence for 2,313 miles from the Canadian border down through the Cascades of Washington and Oregon, the Sierra Nevadas in California and dipping into the desert at the Mexican border. Formal designation by Congress as a National Scenic Trail would serve to upgrade, protect and perpetuate this trail, which follows a route through 25 National Forests, six National Parks, and about 20 per cent through short stretches of private lands.

The Forest Service began surveys of trails in the Cascades and Sierras as early as 1920, but the idea of a border-to-border Pacific Crest Trail was conceived by Clinton C. Clark of Pasadena, California, in 1932. He led in organization of the Pacific Crest Trail Conference, tying together supporters in the three states.

From the Canadian border to the Columbia River, the 457-mile Washington portion is known as the Cascade Crest Trail. It crosses high ridges with views

*Willamette National Forest: Hikers on the Obsidian Trail in the Three Sisters Wilderness Area.*

of snow-covered peaks and glaciers, intersecting historic routes of frontiersmen who broke through the wilderness, including Stevens Pass, Snoqualmie Pass and Cispus Pass. The Klickitat Trail which crosses the Cascade Crest at Cispus is believed to be the first trail in use, since its location by the Indians, between the east and west sides of the high, green Cascades.

At the Columbia River, the trail crosses the Bridge of the Gods and becomes the Oregon Skyline Trail. From the time it climbs out of the Columbia River Gorge, it follows the skyline of the Cascades at elevations from 4,000 to 7,100 feet for a distance of 406 miles across Oregon, winding on the flanks of Mount Hood, through the Mount Jefferson Primitive Area, the Mount Washington Wilderness with its lava flows and basalt columns, and the striking Three Sisters Wilderness.

The California segments are known variously as the Lava Crest Trail, Tahoe Yosemite Trail, John Muir Trail, Sierra Trail and Desert Crest Trail. They cover 1,450 miles in 14 National Forests from the northern end in the Klamath National Forest to the Mexican border just below the Cleveland National Forest and San Diego. But if one spirit imbues these high California footpaths, it is the spirit of John Muir, the master walker and patron saint of walkers, a walker in any season, who found in the Sierra's October the "springtime of snow flowers." These mountains of the Pacific Crest in that season were composed, to him, of "the intense azure of the sky, the purplish grays of the granite, the reds and browns of dry meadows, and the translucent purple and crimson of huckleberry bogs, and the flaming yellow of aspen groves."

John Muir in 1892 founded the Sierra Club, an organization of men and women who have walked in his path, devoting themselves to exploration, enjoyment and protection of the nation's scenic resources, particularly those of mountain regions. The club conducts a series of "Outings" each year for hikers, climbers and for family groups with small children. Some members join clean-up parties, an innovation launched in 1958. With shovels, rakes and can-smashers, the volunteers transform piles of rusted cans strewn at campsites along the trails to a few sackfuls. They burn what debris they can and sack what they cannot for mules

*Many of the rewards of the Sawtooth Primitive Area can be fully appreciated only by travelers on foot.*

119

*Olympic National Forest: Solitary hiker on Quinault Recreation Trail in the luxuriant rain forest.*

*Left: Wilderness hikers in Inyo National Forest view 14,000-foot Sierra Divide and Palisade Glaciers.*

to carry out. They donate their vacations for publicity that calls attention to the problem of litter and focuses on the need for mountain trail manners. Then there are trail maintenance parties, longer and more strenuous than clean-ups, which work under Forest Service supervision in leveling and filling trail beds, making water bars and building retaining walls. On every other day members are free to hike, climb and do as they please.

In Oregon, the Forest Service works with the mountaineering organization known as the Mazamas, organized on the summit of Mount Hood in 1894. The Service seeks advice from standing committees on conservation, research, climbing, trail cutting and skiing, and its personnel put on programs several times a year at meetings. The Mazamas maintain registration boxes on mountain peaks in Oregon, Washington and Mount Shasta in northern California and conduct volunteer trail maintenance in the Columbia Gorge, a part of Mount Hood National Forest.

Similar activities have been conducted jointly between the Forest Service and the Mountaineers, an energetic group founded in Washington State in 1906. A unique creation of the Mountaineers, the Good Outdoor Manners Association, was launched when one of its members, Peggy Robarge, decided the time had come to fight back against vandalism and defacement of National Forests and National Parks. This purely volunteer group, headquartered in Seattle, has conducted a many-sided program built around the symbol of Howdy the Raccoon, the Smokey Bear of trail clean-up in the Northwest. Howdy, GOMA and Peggy Robarge have all been recipients of national awards for their efforts. They have demonstrated not only their right to use the hiking trails, but their devotion to them.

*Hiker's reward: A view of White Water Falls in the Savannah Headwaters area of Pisgah National Forest.*

*There are trails of various kinds in the National Forests, up mountains, through wooded areas and along rivers.*

*Wildflowers along Silver Creek in Arapaho National Forest.*

*Old logging road in White Mountain National Forest, New Hampshire.*

*Rainbow Lake, Beartooth Primitive Area, a special
attraction of the Custer National Forest.*

*Rhododendron in Blackberry Ranger District of
Jefferson National Forest, Virginia.*

*The splendor of Grand Mesa National Forest, Colorado,*
*as seen from Lake View Point.*

*Campsite in the Mount Jefferson Primitive Area in Oregon: A special time for those on a trail overnight comes in the evening.*

# IX | Revolution in Winter Sports

The big crush comes on weekends. Skiers flock to Crystal Mountain, the largest and newest ski center in the Pacific Northwest, in numbers of 4,000 to 6,000 on any crisp, wintry Saturday, returning in almost as strong a force on Sunday. The chalet accommodations provide overnight bunks and beds for a thousand persons and dining for many more. And they are taxed to capacity on a good weekend.

The same holds true in many parts of Oregon and Washington, where 22 per cent of the land lies within National Forest boundaries. Having been established many years ago to protect the headwaters of streams, the Forests logically embrace the high slopes where snows fall early and linger long. As a result, they are the focal points for 90 per cent of various winter sports in the Northwest.

Skiing is a phenomenon of modern times. It was never intended to be a mass sport, or an inexpensive one. No one has tried to make it out to be one. Yet each year it gains more enthusiastic participants, from small children barely able to walk to grandparents; and there is special equipment for one-legged skiers.

The skiing boom began in the East, but seems to have found its glory in the West, where snows are deeper and last longer. In some places, the season begins in November and lasts till April or May. It is estimated that 80 per cent of all the major ski slopes in the West, and some 200 ski areas throughout the country, are located within the National Forests. Some spots provide skiing in sight of the desert. One such is Charleston Peak, in Nevada National Forest, overlooking Las Vegas in one direction and Death Valley in the other. Another is Mount Lemmon Snow Bowl at 9,180 feet in Coronado National Forest, near Tucson, Arizona; it is the country's southernmost ski center, a veritable island of snow high above the desert.

Skiing is found across the National Forest System wherever snows fall. At the opposite end of the continent from Crystal Mountain, both Vermont and New Hampshire have blossomed forth with preeminent ski areas on National Forestland, operated on concession, or "special use" permits. Mount Snow, for instance, is located in the southern district of the Green Mountain National Forest, where one can ski or swim outdoors and skate indoors on the same day.

*Gondola lift carrying skier to top of a run at Sierra Blanca Ski Area, Lincoln National Forest, New Mexico.*

Mount Snow is one of the showplaces of the land of the long white winter, where they used to tell the story of the mailman who would drive his sleigh to the road-side every noon so that his horse could sit atop a telephone pole and rest a while. Another popular spot is Big Bromley, west of Weston, where a double chair-lift ascends the 3,260-foot mountain in eleven minutes. Haystack, Glen Ellen and Corinthia are other areas that are stimulating a tax-producing industry for Vermont, as well as producing outdoor fun for thousands of winter enthusiasts. At Sugarbush Valley, skiers start young, learning from baby-sitters in the pre-junior ski school.

In the White Mountain National Forest, the Italian-designed gondola cars at Wildcat rise 2,000 feet from lower to upper terminal and the start of varying trails and slopes for expert, intermediate and novice. Loon Mountain, off the Kancamagus Highway near Lincoln, is the personal pride of New Hampshire's foremost forester, former Governor Sherman Adams, just as Waterville Valley, one of the greatest new areas in the nation, expressed the taste and touch of its maestro, Olympic skier Tom Corcoran. But for alpine skiing of the old school, nothing compares with Tuckerman Ravine on Mount Washington. There may be no lift facilities in the glacial cirque, but this is the only area in the East where skiing on granular corn snow can be excellent as late as May, and good even in June.

*Right: Mountain climbers making their way slowly up a ridge toward 11,245-foot summit of Mount Hood in Oregon.*

*Below: Ski shelter at Tuckerman Ravine in the White Mountain National Forest, New Hampshire, a major ski area.*

The Forest Service does more than furnish the locale for skiing. It is responsible for the safety of skiers. Forest officers conduct regular inspections of ski lifts and slopes. They collaborate with groups like the Far West Ski Association and Pacific Northwest Ski Association, which not only encourage skiing and improvement in facilities, but ski safety. Snow Rangers are stationed at many heavily used areas, readily identified by their green parkas and black ski pants. One of their major responsibilities is to spot avalanches in the making and to bring them down in controlled slides before they cause serious damage. Modern avalanche control was begun by the Forest Service in 1937 at Alta, Utah (the Wasatch National Forest), in a valley of exciting terrain with a record of frightening snowslide devastation. Through careful testing, the Snow Rangers learned how to precipitate slides, either with dynamite blasts or rifle fire; sometimes the Snow Rangers can trigger an avalanche by crossing steep slopes in early morning long before they are open to the public.

Crystal Mountain is located 76 miles from Seattle high in the Snoqualmie National Forest. From the top of the longest of four chair lifts, it offers a spectacular vantage for viewing its neighboring big brother, Mount Rainier, and the expansive scenery of the Cascades. It also represents a rare experiment in management and ownership of a ski area located entirely on public land. Vail, Sun Valley, Squaw Valley, Crested Butte, Teton Village, Sugarbush and other big names in the skiing world all are corporate operations with their base facilities on private property and their ski slopes under permit from the National Forests. At Crystal Mountain about a thousand skiing families share the financial backing. They put up their money after a long search by energetic ski enthusiasts for a superlative center accessible to Seattle and Portland. They found it here in an isolated high valley sheltered from storms by Mount Rainier. The Forest Service issued a temporary permit provided they could raise working capital. After banks and other sources turned them down, on the grounds it didn't make sense, let alone profit, to build a winter resort in a region of "commuter" skiers, the promoters turned to skiers themselves. For each $1,000 of stock, a skier was promised the opportunity to buy $100 worth of lift tickets for only $10—which seemed a greater inducement than cash dividends. Within five months, $850,000 had been raised.

*Left: Steep headwall of Tuckerman Ravine is recommended only for expert skiers who do not dislike climbing.*

MOST POPULAR SKI AREAS

*Skiers at Big Mountain in the Flathead National Forest, Montana, slip past unusual shapes of snow-covered trees.*

Crystal Mountain opened in 1962 and three years later successfully hosted the National Alpine and National Intercollegiate Championships. These were the greatest winter sports events ever held in the Pacific Northwest and they drew the big names of skiing. Willy Schaeffler set the downhill course. Bob Beattie, the Olympic coach, and Karl Stingl, coach of the University of Washington, greeted teams from schools all over the country, and star competitors of Canada, France, Italy, Austria, England and Switzerland.

The events displayed not only superlative skiing, but a major new ski area. Crystal has steep slopes for racers and experts only, on which even a fair to middling intermediate faces the chance of losing nerve, or "psyching out"; it has bowls, ridges and trails with sufficient variety for all grades of skiers, and cross-country possibilities on the high Cascades. In 1965, the Forest Service approved a $3,500,000 expansion program to include a center for recreation, a chapel, hotel, theatre, tennis courts and skating rink. Perhaps the most unusual facility is the Mountain Top Restaurant, at the 7,800-foot elevation, which skiers and non-skiers reach by chairlifts. From this point, Mount Rainier, draped with its great mantle of glacial ice, looks like a gigantic ice-cream cone almost within reach. The panorama includes in its sweep the Olympics across Puget Sound, Mount Adams, Mount St. Helens, Mount Baker, and other Cascade peaks extending to Mount Hood, near Portland.

Among other major National Forest sites in Washington, White Pass, 125 miles southeast of the Puget Sound region, also offers majestic views of Mount Rainier, as well as the rugged Goat Rocks Wilderness. Stevens Pass, 80 miles east of Seattle, provides a variety of uphill facilities and ski runs. Snoqualmie Summit, the nearest to Seattle (46 miles) is equipped for night skiing. Leavenworth is known for ski-jumping and attracts crowds from all over the Northwest to the annual jumping tournament. Mt. Baker is not only an excellent ski area, with numerous runs and good touring terrain, but a photographer's paradise, being surrounded by Mt. Shuksan and other snowy peaks.

Mount Hood lies roughly midway in the Cascade Range, which extends from Mount Baker, just below the Canadian border in Washington, to Mount Shasta in California. It was born of volcanic eruptions and remains semiactive—on certain days vapor and gas are visible issuing from the crater. After its volcanic formation, the mountain was cleft by glaciers, leaving rivers, canyons and alpine streams in their wake, and almost a dozen active glaciers. In winter, skiers by the thousands swarm beautiful snow-hung trails across the wide slopes. The Timberline course is not considered an advanced or extremely difficult ski course, but it does have one of the longest runs of all, starting from 10,000 feet down to Government Camp, a community six miles below. It also has one of the longest seasons, aided by the use of Sno-cats, which carry skiers to the high reaches of perpetual snow, trampling a few early flowering anemones on the way.

High on the slope of Mount Hood, Timberline Lodge commemorates the best creative performances of those depression-born agencies remembered as the WPA and CCC. The idea of the lodge was conceived by a group of Portland boosters and welcomed by the Government. CCC workers began by hacking and blasting a road. Then it became a fine-arts project, with most of the furniture, striking fabrics and metalcraft pieces hand-made of native materials. In the lobby over the main entrance there is a life-size woodcut of an Oregon mountain lion. Three panels carved of redwood in the main stairway depict the pioneers' trek west. Wood-carvings in relief represent the large animals of the National Forest: black-tailed deer, mule deer, Roose-velt elk, Rocky Mountain elk, black bear and antelope. In 1937, Franklin D. Roosevelt dedicated the massive four-storied, 360-foot long chalet, sheltered by a tre-mendous shingled roof.

Four more ski areas are located at Government Camp, at the 4,000-foot level. A number of ski clubs own their own lodges, built and maintained by summer work parties of their members. Government Camp is the mountain home of the Mazamas, the noted Port-land club of mountaineering conservationists.

Bachelor Butte, one of Oregon's most popular ski areas, affords some of the most spectacular scenery in America. From the tops of the two double chair lifts, high on the face of the lava butte, one can look directly into the open crater of Broken Top Mountain and on to the Three Sisters and other mountain peaks. The perpetual snow fields high on the Butte have served as training grounds for Olympic ski teams. Hoodoo Ski Bowl, at the 4,800-foot level at Santiam Pass in the Central Oregon Cascades, has opportunities for ski touring and snowshoeing nearby. Farther south, the newest winter sports site, Mt. Ashland, also has numer-ous uphill facilities and superb scenic vistas of the Siskiyou Range.

Mechanical aids spurred the skiing revolution: first the rope tow, then the J-bar, T-bar, poma-lift, single chair, double chair, tramway and gondola, saving the skier time and suffering on the uphill climb and allow-ing him more time for the thrills and spills of the descent.

*Returning from a day's skiing on the slopes to the lodge at Missoula Snow Bowl, Lolo National Forest, Montana.*

The activity of skiers, by the very nature of the ski center, is concentrated. It affects choice but small areas of the National Forests; even so, serious questions have been raised as to whether some portions should be developed for such recreation or conserved in their natural forms.

In the late 1950's and 1960's a new revolution, also mechanically induced, swept over the winter outdoors scene. It was the beginning of the age of a new gadget called the snowmobile, and where it would lead, for better or worse, no one could rightly say.

The most popular type of snowmobile has ski-like runners in the front, is steered like a motorcycle by handle bars and driven by a rear track. The track, powered by a small engine, is similar to a miniature tank tread with ice cleats. But unlike a tank the average snowmobile hits speeds of 30 to 50 miles an hour on ice or snow, while racing machines reach 85 miles an hour.

These vehicles caught on first in Canada, where they were used by hunters, trappers and loggers. Then snow-cruising clubs began springing up in both Canada and the United States. At Peterborough, Ontario, an estimated 20,000 spectators watched 400 racers compete for the Kawartha Cup in 1965. Thirty manufacturers moved into the field, adding more powerful engines, new drive tracks, more passenger comfort, and adver-

tising the thrills of riding the wind at tingling speeds with much the same exhilaration found in motorcycles and bobsleds.

In early 1968 an estimated 100,000 or more snow-mobiles were in use. The prospect of a million within five years did not appear too unlikely.

Their drivers would include all age groups, some in poor physical condition, some improperly clothed, with little knowledge of winter travel. Nevertheless, an article in a camping magazine generously encouraged all comers. "The question everyone immediately asks," according to the article, "after hearing of the potential fun and adventure the snowmobiles induce is, where can these machines be used? The answer: virtually anywhere."

This, however, was not precisely the case. The article did not mention that the Forest Service had been obliged to train one Smokejumper unit as a winter rescue group, which in 1966 had parachuted to furnish assistance to two stranded snowmobile parties until they could be hauled out. Nor did it mention that snowmobiles are not permitted in wilderness areas.

*Gallatin National Forest, Montana: Snowmobiling is the newest winter sport in the National Forests.*

The snowmobiler still had a very large area open to him with minimum restrictions on public lands. Places considered inaccessible only a few years earlier were on the brink of becoming winter playgrounds.

But questions were still to be answered at the dawn of the snowmobile age.

For instance, the snowmobile is apt to expose the user to the most hazardous terrain, in the canyon bottoms, where tons of snow pile up when an avalanche comes to rest. And when conditions are most critical, a slight disturbance may be all that it takes to trigger an avalanche of major proportions. Should the snowmobiler be permitted unrestricted access to such areas?

On long distance travel into remote areas, if the snowmobile breaks down or the driver gets lost or caught in a sudden winter storm, there is serious danger of exposure and disaster. Should filing a trip plan be required, as well as carrying emergency equipment for survival?

Snow provides a handy receptacle for disposing of empty fuel containers and other litter, which become exposed the following spring and mar the landscape. Can snowmobilers be guided to burn all combustible refuse and pack out all other items, as wilderness users

*Right: Chairlift at Mount Alyeska in the Chugach National Forest, Alaska, is silhouetted by setting sun.*

do? Should toilets and sanitation facilities be developed for snowmobilers?

Game animals find sanctuary in winter solitude. They struggle to survive through the season and are especially weak in February and March. Should areas they frequent be open to snowmobile use?

The Forest Service in the late 1960's embarked on a program of marking safe snowmobile trails, on the theory that if trails are interesting and well-planned, a majority of the users will spend their time on them. The more venturesome doubtless will leave the trails, but usually not until they have experience in touring and some knowledge of avalanche hazard, thin ice and weather conditions.

There is no telling where snowmobiling will go. It is great fun for those who have tried it and it is here to stay. Who can tell, it may in time lead to appreciation of the wonders of the winter world, and this could yet prove its most important role.

*Missoula Snow Bowl: The great increase in the number of skiers recently began in the East but now is more pronounced in the West.*

# X | Land of Grass

Before the land was settled, a sea of grass spread between the Western deserts and the forests of the East.

Grass, though a humble plant, provided sustenance to wild animals that dominated the Great Plains and broad intermountain ranges. The land supported bison and antelope in fantastic numbers. In those former times, fertility was insured by nature's cycles.

These regions were destined for grass. In the long course of geologic history, the Western plains were raised to their present elevations, usually 2,500 feet or more above sea level. Mountain ranges were thrust even higher and these now intercept most of the rain and snow.

The plains receive less than 20 inches of rainfall a year. And the wind blows relentlessly, harder and longer than in any other part of the country. On such high, windy plains grass survives well. But other plants must struggle to survive.

Now the grasslands have been altered by the course of settlement. But all animals—the man that now stands dominant, his domestic stock and the animals that endure in the wild—are still dependent on the power of grass. They are dependent on man's ability to use the grass without depleting or destroying the nutrients of the soil from which it comes.

About 60,000 farmer-rancher families graze livestock in the National Forests and National Grasslands under permit. They own land, livestock, buildings and other properties that form part of the American rural landscape, of sky and grass and cattle, of fences and ponds and wells. Most of the farms and ranches on National Forest System lands are small family operations; their net incomes average less than $3,000 annually.

Their cattle and sheep are also found sometime during the year on more than 100 million acres of natural range environment of National Forests and National Grasslands. Most National Forest System grazing occurs in the mountainous areas—the high alpine meadows of the West—but it also extends across the plains to the tidal marshes and coastal piney woods of the South.

The length of time livestock are allowed to graze on the range may be four months or less where the growing season is short and vegetation and soils are delicate, or virtually all year where climate is mild and suitable for plant growth. The season for cattle averages under five months, the season for sheep under two and a half months.

*Little Missouri National Grasslands, North Dakota:*
*Gullies in foreground show result of abrasive action of silt.*

At the time when the Forest Reserves were created from the public domain, much of the land was already heavily grazed. Overuse had led to range deterioration. The valuable grasses had thinned and disappeared. "The general lack of control," reported the Public Lands Commission of 1905, "has resulted, naturally and inevitably, in overgrazing and the ruin of millions of acres of otherwise valuable grazing territory. Lands useful for grazing are losing their only capacity for productiveness, as of course they must when no legal control is exercised." The need for an orderly process in administering range use was clearly evident.

Never before in the history of any nation had constructive methods been applied to protect the forage cover on lands in public ownership. Very little, indeed, had been done along these lines on private lands. The problems of the period called for an overturning of ideas, a new science, a new field of adventure. The grazing permit system was established in 1905 as the first step. The range reconnaissance in 1910 in the Coconino National Forest of Arizona was a forward stride in determining capacity to be balanced with use.

Through the years, permittees, or groups of permittees, have been assigned areas called grazing allotments, of which there were more than 11,600 in 1967. In some cases sharp reductions have been made in the numbers of cattle or sheep on allotments. In other cases, watershed cover has been improved and forage production increased (for livestock and wildlife) through intensive grazing management and seeding—or a combination of the two. During 1967, almost a quarter-million acres of depleted rangeland were revegetated and 1,200 water developments for livestock and wildlife were installed.

But the Forest Service and its permittees have learned that management must be a many-sided, long range venture. These lands are of high value to the nation. The rangeland environment provides a home during most of the year for millions of wild animals. It provides a regulated flow of high-quality water to farms and cities. It yields benefits of recreation, mental uplift and physical improvement to millions of visitors. All these, as well as providing forage for meat production, and contributing to the natural beauty and economic stability of rural communities.

*Panhandle National Grassland, Texas: This area, part of the dust bowl in the 1930's, now has good grass cover.*

*Badlands terrain in Little Missouri National Grasslands, an area of over a million acres in North Dakota.*

"We still have a terrific backlog of work to do," declared Edward P. Cliff, Chief of the Forest Service, before the American Society of Range Management in 1967. "For example, there are 54,000 miles of range fences on the National Forests; another 60,000 miles are needed. We have 38,000 livestock watering developments; we need another 37,000. We have rehabilitated 2.5 million acres of deteriorated range; another 7.6 million acres need rehabilitation . . . .

"Watershed values are becoming more and more important in area after area. Neither the livestock industry nor the Forest Service can live with grazing practices that result in damage to watersheds. Maintaining an adequate plant cover must be one of the measures of our performance."

Thus grass must remain. Grass is the key to a whole system of agriculture. Protection and perpetuation of grass is the difference between success and failure for holding soils in place, for development of economic strength in rural communities, and for social benefits on a wide scale.

The 19 National Grasslands are located in 11 Western states—17 on the Great Plains, one each in Idaho and Oregon—and they cover nearly four million acres of Federal land, all consecrated to the way of life which is based on grass.

143

*A dragonfly alights in his customary sunny place near stream in Mark Twain National Forest.*

*Turnagain Pass, 65 miles southeast of Anchorage, Alaska, in Chugach National Forest.*

*Kaniksu National Forest, Idaho: Moon over Priest Lake highlights fall colors.*

*Indian paintbrush in Bird Creek Meadows, Gifford Pinchot National Forest.*

*Above: Canadian River flows through Mills Canyon in Panhandle National Grassland where red sandstone outcroppings appear.*

*The season of sprightly colors along the Apache Trail, Tonto National Forest, Arizona.*

The stockmen of the early cattle drives used parts of this land, but without thought of management. Then the farmers came. They began with trouble and lived as partners with trouble as long as they tried to farm grass country. Few could make a decent living on a 160-acre homestead in the high plains. They eked out a meagre subsistence on poor lands unsuited for intensive cultivation, and with insufficient rainfall. They were utterly ruined by depressed crop prices of the 1930's, recurrent drought, excessive grazing, and relentless winds that changed sod to dust. Ten-foot drifts of snow, unimpeded by natural ground cover stopped highway and rail traffic. People lost their ways in blizzards a hundred yards from home. Two dust storms blew 2,000 miles to pass over the nation's capital, almost blotting out the sun, and then settling on the decks of ships 300 miles offshore in the Atlantic Ocean. To this day some areas still bear the scars of a thoughtless past. Dust blows and gullies gnaw at lands on abandoned farms. In place of grass, sage and short-lived scrawny cheat grass shape the landscape. The land was impoverished, and the people were impoverished. The people fled, but the land remained.

In the 1930's, the Resettlement Administration purchased submarginal farms by the thousands and helped farm families to find new opportunities elsewhere. The areas purchased were slowly rehabilitated. Land Utilization Projects, as they came to be known, brought grassland agriculture to the Western plains and restored grass to its place as the dominant vegetative resource.

The genius of this movement was the late Dr. Hugh Bennett, founder of the Soil Conservation Service and one of the foremost conservationists in American history. The areas remained under his agency as demonstration projects until 1953, when they were transferred to several Federal and state agencies. Of the lands assigned to the Forest Service, about four million acres were given permanent status in 1960 and incorporated into the National Forest System. They ceased being known by their former name, Land Utilization Projects, and became National Grasslands—sister areas of the National Forests.

The comeback of grassland is a notable story in American land husbandry. Ponds and lakes, the work of men rather than nature, hold rainfall and snowmelt for the dry season. Their scattered locations disperse cattle evenly over the range. Miles of fences line the road or march out across the open plain, dividing the range into units that also distribute livestock grazing. Fences often protect marshy areas on the ponds where waterfowl and wildlife nest and feed.

At the end of the fall mating season, herds of mule deer now can move down from their forested summer ranges in the mountains, to the lower winter regions, where they feed on grasses and shrubs such as bitterbrush and sagebrush. And in the spring there will be

*Below: Another view of Mills Canyon, from canyon floor. Above: Pasture for guest ranch in Lewis and Clark National Forest.*

tender green grasses for the deer before they climb back to the high places.

The land is open. Animals have the room they need for running—particularly the swift pronghorn, which is found nowhere in the world outside North America and bespeaks the glory of the grassland life community. Subsisting on grasses, forbs and shrubs, in places like Thunder Basin National Grassland, Wyoming, it has rebuilt its population after being near extinction a few decades ago. Though its legendary herds are now gone, it ranks second in number only to deer as a big game animal in Wyoming. Thunder Basin is also coming into its own as a national asset for its geological formations containing deposits of late cretaceous dinosaurs.

No other region contains such a variety of upland birds as the plains. Native sage grouse and quail are common species; so is the beautiful Hungarian partridge. Waterfowl find the prairie lakes and ponds attractive after their long annual flights from the north. Many waterfowl, in fact, are produced at waterholes on the prairie.

In the rolling prairie of the Cimarron National Grassland, in the extreme southwest corner of Kansas, prime consideration is given to protecting and restoring the habitat of the rare lesser prairie chicken, which has its nesting grounds here. This grassland astride the Cimarron River is rich in historic resources, as an ancient hunting ground of the Kiowa and Comanche Indians and as a pathway for the Santa Fe Trail, the ruts of which are still plainly visible in many sections.

Another interesting National Grassland, Pawnee, in the northern portion of Colorado's Great Plains, is composed of high buttes and distant horizons, with many places suited for the restoration of prairie dog towns. And in the Badlands of North Dakota, the Little Missouri Grassland embraces part of the historic area which Theodore Roosevelt knew during his days as a young rancher.

For at least a generation these sections were virtually lost to the nation, infertile, unproductive and desolate. Their restoration is now being marked by their rediscovery and a new usefulness in the land of grass.

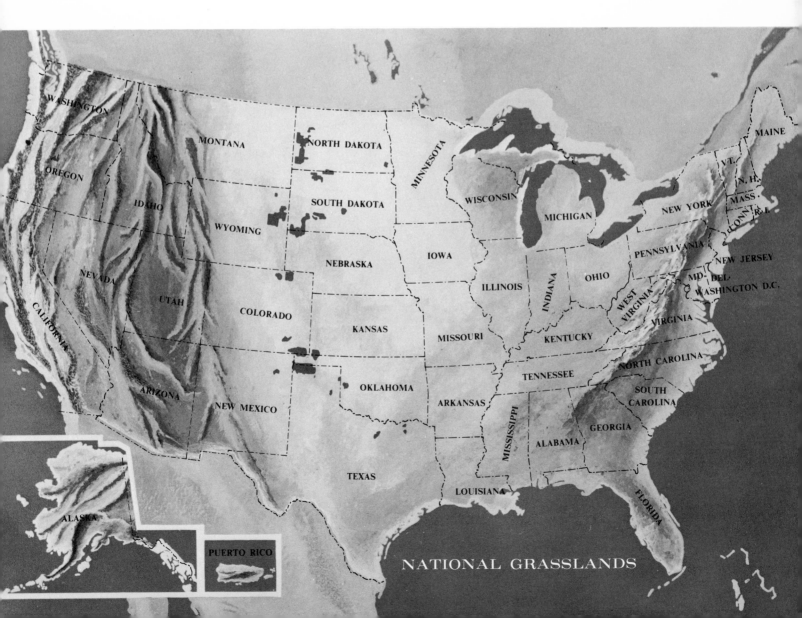

NATIONAL GRASSLANDS

# XI | National Forests in the Alaska of Tomorrow

Alaska is very likely the portion of North America longest inhabited by man. Its beginnings are traceable to the age of Beringia, the ancient land bridge which the Wandering Hunters crossed from Asia, thus introducing the higher form of life to this continent.

Alaska is also the newest portion of North America, second youngest of the 50 states, the least developed and the least spoiled. Its naturalness is one of the marvels of the modern world, and therefore a special prize of all the nation.

The National Forests, in turn, are among the oldest and newest parts of Alaska. They date from 1892, when President Harrison proclaimed the establishment of Afognak Island Forest and Fish Culture Reserve as one of the first withdrawals from the public domain following the authorization granted by Congress the preceding year. The balance of the lands were added during the Roosevelt-Pinchot era of 1902-1909.

But for many years the National Forestlands of Alaska were remote and inaccessible, and the role of the Forest Service largely custodial. Two main developments of recent times (since the Statehood Act of 1958) are responsible for great changes in the role of the National Forests. First, large scale logging has become a practicality, affording opportunities to fully utilize and manage the wood resource for the first time. Second, the "marine highway," consisting of big and efficient car-carrying ferries operated by the state, has opened unlimited opportunities for National Forest outdoor adventures. Add to this the nearness of Alaska in the jet age—Juneau lies 900 miles from Seattle or less than two hours by plane—and isolation has clearly ended.

The two National Forests, the Tongass and Chugach, cover about six per cent of Alaska's total land. The huge Tongass, a domain over 500 miles long, up to 100 miles wide and covering 16 million acres, is by far the largest National Forest anywhere in the country. Second in size is the Chugach, with five million acres.

The National Forests embrace most of the coastal woodlands of temperate southeast Alaska, which are

*Forest flora of Point Gustavus is covered with ferns, mosses and lichens. It is already apparent that the young stand of Sitka spruce is being followed by hemlock.*

150

*The famous Mendenhall Glacier as seen from across Mendenhall Lake. The peak in the background is 5,250-foot Mount Stroller.*

really an extension of the Pacific Northwest rain forest. Over half the National Forest land is composed of islands, while the mainland portion is deeply cleft by bays, inlets and large rivers, creating thousands of miles of shoreline. These are the kinds of highly scenic, misty and moody places the ferries bring into range. The big ships first began operation in 1963 to link the isolated villages of the southeast—Ketchikan, Wrangell, Petersburg, Sitka, Juneau, Haines and Skagway. Except for the last two, at the northern end, they had no rail or highway connection to the outside world. The same year National Forestland around Cordova became accessible with the ferry from Valdez. And the following year Afognak could be reached when service was opened between Kodiak Island and the mainland.

The design and destiny of southeast Alaska and the National Forests are intimately joined, in past, present and future. The Chugach was the site of Alaska's discovery by Vitus Bering, the intrepid Russian commander who, with his shipmates of 1741, sighted Eskimo camps on Kayak and Wingham Islands, both within today's boundaries of the Chugach. Further south, Sitka, now surrounded by the Tongass (except on the Pacific side), subsequently became the capital of Russian America, and headquarters of Alexander Baranof, "Lord of Alaska," until the Seward Purchase of 1867. Now Sitka is reachable by ferry on a voyage from Juneau through island-dotted channels; and almost adjacent to the ferry terminal lies the Forest Service Starrigavan Campground, from whence one can (and should) drive upward through alpine meadows to Harbor Mountain for a view of Sitka's harbor and the blue Pacific.

The fascination in glaciers lies in the dynamics of movement, the visible and invisible, that remind the viewer that nothing on this revolving earth can be stationary or static and that natural law shall always take precedence over human law.

*Above: Aerial view looking south across South Sawyer Glacier shows two other rivers of ice joining the main glacier.*

*Left: Portage Glacier, 50 miles from Anchorage, is six and a half miles long, three-quarters of a mile wide, and its face is 80 feet high.*

Southeast Alaska has the largest glaciers on earth outside of Greenland and Antarctica. In this region, 175 glaciers are large enough to be named. They are born where heavy precipitation in the form of snow accumulates over the years without summer thaw. The snow compacts into ice and the ice flows down the valleys to return to the sea.

Perhaps the most spectacular sight of the National Forests is the Tracy Arm, a 30-mile long indented waterway, south of Juneau, flanked by sheer rock walls like a Norwegian fjord. Mountain goats can be spotted navigating among the crags, and hundreds of seals and sea lions can be seen swimming among bluish icebergs, splintered off the towering icy parapet of Sawyer Glacier. Cruises from Juneau sail up the Tracy Arm, and charter sightseeing planes skim over—and between—the 2,000-foot-high rock walls.

The visitor learns to look at Alaskan glaciers from diverse angles and to read the history of the earth in the grooves showing direction of movement; the scoured and polished outcrops of bedrock; the topography sculptured by the ice, and the revegetation in newly uncovered soil and rock.

*The most striking aspect of native art in Alaska is the totem pole, some of which are 30 to 100 feet high.*

The terminus of Mendenhall Glacier, a few miles outside of Juneau, is the most photographed glacial attraction in Alaska, perhaps because Mendenhall is easily accessible by road. Over 100,000 visitors a year come to the dramatic Mendenhall Visitor Center, commanding a three-dimensional view of the glacial edge of the massive Juneau Ice Field. However, more questions than answers are provided by scale models, telescopic viewers and lectures, for Mendenhall is a receding glacier, losing ground to invading lichens and mosses at an average rate of 90 feet a year, while the Taku and almost a dozen others continue to advance. Scientists who have been tracking the climate and glacial movements of the 1,200-square-mile Juneau Ice Field, one of the most sensitive on earth, since 1946 feel that by the turn of the next century Mendenhall may reverse its movement, driving mountain goats from their rocky cliffs to the valleys and forcing human dwellers down below to adjust as well.

Meanwhile campers can set up quarters in a field of wildflowers (which 50 years ago was under ice), with loons and Arctic terns as neighbors in Mendenhall Lake. And there, in the long, slow summer twilight, they can watch the glacial face fade from bluish white to whitish blue and then darken in the shadows as it bids them goodnight.

In the Chugach National Forest, mountain peaks, glaciers, lakes and streams comprise other stages in the continuous performance of land-shaping, which is sometimes gentle and subtle and other times violence personified, like the earthquake of Good Friday, 1964, which cracked the earth in jigsaw fashion, reshaped a shoreline, submerged dry land and laid glacier faces flat. The focal point, the Portage Glacier, 50 miles southeast of Anchorage and beyond Alaska's most popular ski center, Mt. Alyeska, is the scene of high winds that rip and tear at vegetation and give a storm-wrought appearance to the scene. The glacier is fast receding, about 200 feet a year, with icebergs peeling off and splashing into Portage Lake.

Art forms are implicit in the natural landscape of Alaska, in the mist-shrouded low lying coasts, the birds outlined in flight against a mass of snow, the composition of sky, forest, sea and tundra. In the native peoples, the Indians and Eskimos, who comprise one-fourth the population of the state, vibrant earthly art is deep-rooted, rich and complex, having served since antiquity in utilitarian, ornamental, ceremonial, philosophical and religious expressions. The genius of these peoples created a panoply of arts, out of wood, feathers, minerals, shells and ivory, and, in the case of the coastal Indians, they were so rich in resources that they gave away their treasures at the feasts called potlatches.

*Beyond Auke Lake is Mendenhall Glacier, easily accessible by road and the most photographed glacial attraction in Alaska.*

Their great totems, decorative records of outstanding events in the life of family or clan, virtually disappeared under the pressures of time and the white man's ways. One of the first attempts to rescue the surviving masterworks was made during the 1930's by the Civilian Conservation Corps under the direction of B. Frank Heintzleman, Regional Forester (and later territorial governor). Poles were found in scattered settlements, many in seldom visited canoe harbors, and then were assembled in communities where descendants of the old master carvers now reside: New Kasaan, Saxman and Totem Bight, near Ketchikan, Kydaburg, Klawak, Wrangell and Sitka. In more recent times, the neighboring communities of Haines and Port Chilkoot have been the center of an effort to preserve and perpetuate the arts and crafts of the Tlingit Indians.

The dark coastal forests, glacial flats and waters that inspired the Indian artists are still rich in fish, birds and mammals to be interpreted by artists still to come.

The Copper River Delta, spread across 330,000 acres of silt and gravel washed down from the Copper River near Cordova, is one of the outstanding waterfowl nesting areas on the entire continent. It not only supports the largest known population of huge trumpeter swans, but thousands of Western Canada geese, pintails, widgeons and mallards. And during the spring and fall these are joined by thousands more migrating waterfowl and shorebirds.

*(Continued on page 160)*

*A growth of fireweed in wild Summit Lake country, Chugach National Forest, Alaska.*

*Forest Service launch in fjord-like inlet of the Tongass National Forest, Alaska.*

*Tongass National Forest: Spectacular view from Harbor Mountain of Sitka Sound.*

*Fall run of silver salmon in Whitewater Creek, Admiralty Island, Tongass National Forest.*

*Above: Most of the totem poles restored in the National Forests of Alaska have been set up in clusters accessible to visitors.*

*The peaks of the Kenai Mountains are reflected in small, nameless lake in Chugach National Forest.*

The old mining country between Resurrection and Juneau Creek is known for its concentration of big game—from this region hunters have taken some of the largest trophy moose, with antler spreads over six feet, as well as Dall sheep, mountain goat and black bear. The Yakutat area is noted among hunters for its large and growing moose herd. Afognak Island supports the original elk herd in Alaska, the descendants of a handful transplanted from the Olympic Peninsula in 1929. Clear mountain streams and lakes are rich in several species of trout and during the spawning periods these fresh waters become cradles of new life for anadromous trout and salmon that come in from the ocean to lay and fertilize their eggs. Indeed, one of the principal missions of the National Forests is to protect the habitat for salmon, which constitutes an important economic resource for Alaska, as well as a source of pleasure for sport fishermen, and of food for bears and bald eagles.

Most of the fjords, high mountain lakes and beaches lie in the wilderness, far beyond the end of the road. At more than 100 such settings the National Forests maintain furnished and equipped cabins for public use. Most are reached only by plane. They help to increase hunting where overpopulation may exist and supply the kind of solitude that fishermen dream about. They also afford anyone a taste of the Alaskan wilderness. The A-frame cabin at Shelikoff Bay, north of Sitka, lies only a stone's throw from a beautiful black sand beach on the Pacific shore. Visitors to the Redoubt Lake cabin, on Baranof Island, may find a hummingbird staging a performance of perpetual motion outside the window, while geese and gulls flock around a cascading waterfall in the distance. Two cabins are located on Hasselborg Lake, whose clear and blue waters extend six miles or more in a cradle of mountains on Admiralty Island.

Admiralty constitutes a special province. It lies almost within view of Juneau and has been a center of public attention for many years. The principal focus has been on providing a sanctuary for the island's substantial population of Alaska brown bears, the largest land mammal on the continent. Protecting the bears also involves protecting the streams; bears eat many foods but they are champion fishermen and their staple is salmon. Admiralty is also a prime habitat for bald eagles which are found in hundreds of nests along the many beaches.

Admiralty is 100 miles long, 25 miles wide at its widest and comprises a million acres. The heavy rainfall nurtures the dark forests of spruce and hemlock, and these, too, constitute valuable resources. Parts of the island have been logged for many years, but the current demand for timber and the opportunity for heavy cutting represent a challenge never faced before. Nevertheless, two-thirds of the island are to be maintained free of any timber cutting under Forest Service plans. In order to assure protection of salmon streams from

*Rocky cliffs along fjord-like Tracy Arm rise steeply from water's edge to elevations of 3,000 feet and more.*

sedimentation and disturbance caused by logging or road building, these plans provide for regular inspections by Forest Service and State Fisheries biologists of areas where cutting is permitted. Not only on Admiralty, but throughout the Tongass and Chugach the step-up in logging emphasizes the need for priority attention to protection and management of wildlife.

What really lies in the tomorrow of Alaska, of which these expansive National Forestlands are part?

"We must meet the challenge of Alaska," the late John F. Kennedy declared in 1960. "We must be careful to avoid the same piecemeal, uncoordinated, wasteful approach which has too often characterized our resource development in the past."

To these lines may be added the prayer of Mrs. Margaret Murie, who gave to Alaska her childhood, her youth as the first woman graduate of the university, the years of her life as companion in pioneering explorations with her distinguished naturalist husband, the late Olaus Murie: "that Alaska will not lose the heart-nourishing friendliness of her youth—that her people will always care for one another, her towns remain friendly and not completely ruled by the dollar—and that her great wild places will remain great, and wild, and free, where wolf and caribou, wolverine and grizzly bear, and all the arctic blossoms may live on in the delicate balance which supported them long before impetuous man appeared in the North."

*Right: Another view of Tracy Arm showing where it meets South Sawyer Glacier. Remnant of the glacier that carved valley in upper half of picture can be seen in background.*

# XII | On the Trails of History

William Bartram was a singular explorer, whose adventures are noteworthy in the fields of natural history, history, American and English literature, philosophy and religion. For four years, starting in 1773, he probed the wilderness of the Carolinas, Georgia, Alabama and Florida, south to the Gulf of Mexico and as far west as the Mississippi. It was a monumental journey. Occasionally he would emerge at a trading post or seaport to pick up provisions or drop off plant specimens. But for months on end he was out of touch with his civilization, visiting, studying and befriending the Cherokee, Creek, Seminole (who called him Puc Puggy, "Flower Hunter"), Chickasaw and Choctaw. Mostly he was alone, a wandering Robinson Crusoe, at home in the wilds, collecting the source materials for his classic work, now called *The Travels of William Bartram*, living in his own style of "primeval simplicity and honesty," as one admiring scientist later described it.

One of his most exciting trips led from Charleston, South Carolina, into the high Appalachians, the country of the Cherokee. He stopped at Indian villages and botanized in a wide arc. It was on this trip that the flame azalea, spreading across the ascending hillsides, evoked from Bartram one of the loveliest and most renowned botanical descriptions: "The epithet fiery I annex to this celebrated species of Azalea, as being expressive of the appearance in flower." It seemed to him that the clusters of the blossoms cover the shrubs in such profusion "that suddenly opening to view from dark shades, we are alarmed with the apprehension of the hills being set on fire. This is certainly the most gay and brilliant flowering shrub yet known."

After riding through spacious high forests and flowery meadows, he arrived at Nantahala Gorge. In the distance ahead, descending from the heights, he saw a band of Indians riding rapidly toward him, and presently met their chieftain. This encounter is recorded on the upper rim of Nantahala Gorge, within Nantahala National Forest. The Nantahalas have a glory of their own. They were a favorite Cherokee hunting ground and are still popular for bear, boar and deer. The rugged mountains are forested with oak, tulip-poplar, pine, basswood, many species of shrubs and trees and include 50 miles of the Appalachian Trail. The Gorge is surrounded by mile-high peaks, its slopes forested with hemlock. And there a historical marker reads:

WILLIAM BARTRAM
Philadelphia Naturalist, Author,
exploring this area met a Cherokee
band led by their Chief Attakullakulla,
in May, 1775, near this spot.

The National Forests everywhere are filled with such historic and literary landmarks, of old iron furnaces, ghost towns, cliff dwellings, battlegrounds, ruts of wagon trails, trails of explorers that lead from Bartram in the east to Lewis and Clark at the western edge of the continent.

The "historical resource" has always been there, but current times in the National Forests have been marked with a new awakening, of cultivating the past through research, preservation, restoration and interpretation, thus affording use of the land as a valuable, living document of history.

In Kentucky, a whole National Forest was renamed in 1966 from Cumberland to the Daniel Boone in honor of the wilderness pioneer. Americans can turn back the pages of time and see forests being restored to conditions in which Boone found them two centuries ago. The unique Pioneer Weapons Hunting Area, covering 7,300 acres, is designed specially for old-time weapons—longbow, crossbow, flintlock rifle and percussion cap rifle. The flintlock was companion to the pioneer, the percussion cap to the western scout, Civil War trooper and Indian fighter. With these weapons, sportsmen face a real test in hunting squirrels, the old favorite of the Kentucky woods, and wild turkey, king of game birds (which once virtually disappeared with the buffalo), as well as deer, grouse, foxes, and rabbits.

Much is still being learned about Daniel Boone. In 1962, in a hidden spot deep in a gorge in the National Forest, three hikers discovered a rude cabinlike structure made without use of a single nail. They found a board inscribed with the lettering "D BooN," which authorities later said looked much like other famous carvings of the old frontiersman. Near the shelterhouse they found remains of stone furnaces and part of a trough adzed out of a poplar log, and a small iron pot such as pioneers used in cooking over an open fire.

It has been suggested that the site may have been the mining and smelting location used by John Swift, the mysterious figure who fathered the folk legend of Swift's Silver Mine and who may have lured Boone on his scouting trips with notions of wealth. After its discovery, the National Forest staff endeavored, for the time being, to protect the site from vandalism by keeping its location secret, permitting access only to scholars who might help unravel its meaning.

Iron furnaces are scattered about the National Forests of the East and Midwest.

"Give 'er fire!"—this cry rang through woods more than a century ago as busy colliers tended huge piles of wood burning into charcoal to be used as fuel by the ironmaster and helpers. Crude conical huts, each with wood stove and rough log bunks, were home to these men, who tended as many as nine pits at a time, all of which demanded constant watching during the ten days to two weeks it took for them to "burn off."

What was once the Elizabeth Furnace Community—a bustling 19th-century settlement that made its living from the iron and wood resources of the Massanutten Mountains of Virginia—is now part of the George Washington National Forest. To tell the story of the Elizabeth Furnace, the National Society of the Children of the American Revolution and the Forest Service cooperated in a partial restoration and development of the Pig Iron Trail.

In the mid-1830's it was one of eight furnaces operating in the Massanuttens and nearby Shenandoah Mountains. The big bellows pumped up and down, flames from the furnace lit up the night sky, and ton after ton of molten iron ran into casting beds of sand. In the fall, when the furnace run was over, many of the furnacemen took to the forests and mountains to make their living by mining the brown iron ore or felling trees for charcoal. Wood had to be cut year-round, for the furnace consumed 600 bushels of charcoal a day.

Its last years were the 1880's. Furnaces using coke rather than charcoal were producing enormous quantities of iron inexpensively and mass production was making much of the work of the local blacksmith obsolete. Even the most faithful customers eventually turned to distant manufacturing firms for their iron products. There the story of these furnaces ended until the recent restoration.

During the Civil War, Elizabeth Furnace was part of the network that made Virginia known as the "Arsenal of the South." Farther west (and north), the iron and charcoal industry of the Hanging Rock region of Ohio, near Ironton on the Ohio River, influenced the industrial life of the nation. Reportedly there were three areas in the world then capable of producing high quality iron for heavy cannon. Two were in Europe, the third was the Hanging Rock region. The hulls of the *Monitor* and *Merrimac* and the big guns of Harpers Ferry began as glowing metal in furnaces of the region.

Vesuvius, now within the Wayne National Forest, was one of the first iron blast furnaces of Hanging Rock. Built in 1833, it started with charcoal and air—a cold blast principle—but a more efficient process, the hot blast, was developed soon afterward. In the late nineties, in the twilight of its years, Vesuvius reverted to the cold blast before banking its fires for the last time in 1906. The stonework and setting of the furnace have been restored by the Vesuvius Job Corps Conservation Center, a historic unit of the Lake Vesuvius Recreation Area.

In Illinois, the first furnace of record was built in 1839 four miles northwest of Elizabethtown. In due course it was enlarged and during the Civil War served

*Chief Forester Edward P. Cliff at ceremony at recently renamed Daniel Boone National Forest.*

as an important source of iron for the U. S. Navy. The furnace tract became part of Shawnee National Forest in 1950.

By 1966 it was in poor condition, beyond repair. In one of the largest Job Corps projects, the entire structure was dismantled and reassembled, stone by stone. The Illinois Furnace, like the original, stands 42 feet high, tapering upward from its 32-foot-square base.

In the same National Forest, the George Rogers Clark Recreation Way, stretching over 100 miles across the Shawnee Hills, has been proposed as a means of conserving and interpreting ancient Indian mounds and the movements of George Rogers Clark and his men on their Revolutionary War advance on Kaskaskia.

From the age of the early blast furnaces, the nation moved westward into an age of search for gold and silver, in which Colorado had its years of glory. A vestige of that heyday is the last regularly scheduled narrow-gauge passenger train, the Silverton. It runs during the summer from Durango to Silverton through the San Juan National Forest to give a sentimental glimpse of those rugged times when the railroad linked remote mining towns with the outside world.

The puffing, coal-burning engine trailed by brightly colored coaches is operated by the Denver & Rio

*Red oak shake, carved with words "D BooN," was found leaning against primitive hut in National Forest by three Kentuckians exploring Red River country in 1959.*

Grande Railroad; the Forest Service cooperates with signs along the way identifying points of historical interest, streams, peaks high above the steep canyon walls, and old mines and ghost towns clinging to the mountainsides. The train chugs and clicks along the Animas River, which the Spanish explorers named Rio de las Animas Perdidas, or "River of Lost Souls."

Recorded history of what is now the National Forest dates back to 1765, when Captain Juan Marie de Rivera and his party reached the San Juan Basin on an expedition from Santa Fe. Father Francisco Escalante, who followed the next year, named geographical and topographical features, many of which are still retained.

Fur trappers and mountain men followed the trails of the Spaniards into southwestern Colorado. One important expedition from the St. Louis Fur Company brought a heavy influx of trappers in 1831. Lured by the dream of wealth in gold and silver, the prospectors came next. And the last to stake their claims to the San Juan Basin were the cattlemen and sheepmen. The National Forest covers more than two million acres, and bears traces of every group.

The heart of the fur-trapping empire, however, was not in Colorado, but in Wyoming. Bernard DeVoto described the Western fur trade in his book, *Across the Wide Missouri*, which focuses on the Green River Rendezvous, held among Indians and trappers each spring at the foot of the Wind River Mountains.

This was Jim Bridger country. The National Forest on the western flank of the Wind Rivers is named for him. Opinion and estimates of Jim Bridger vary, but generals for whom he scouted said he knew every mountain peak, deep gorge and stream of the West. As a youngster of seventeen, he first came to this corner of Wyoming with General William Ashley's Rocky Mountain Fur Company in 1823. In the next 20 years, rawboned, gray-eyed "Old Gabe" discovered many of the landmarks in what now are National Forests between the Rockies and the Sierras. He ranged north to Canada, west to the Pacific, but every summer found him back in this country. In the cottonwood flats where the Green River and Horse Creek meet, Captain Benjamin Bonneville had built his log fort in 1832; from then on, the valley became the nerve center of Western mountain fur trade. From 1833 to 1837 (except for '34), the annual rendezvous was held here. Dr. Marcus Whitman, who pioneered the Oregon Trail, came to the rendezvous of 1835, and, in a very delicate operation, removed an Indian arrowhead which had been imbedded in Jim Bridger's back. Every year the citizens of Pinedale recreate the rendezvous, with the cooperation of the Forest Service and other agencies and with all the main characters represented.

If one rides or hikes up into the Jim Bridger Wilderness, he comes to Trapper and Little Trapper Lakes, favorites of the early trappers and reminders of their role in opening the West. They blazed trails, located water and grass, named the lakes and rivers. On the less romantic side, as DeVoto pointed out, the wealth they produced went east into other hands and stayed there.

*Visitors at one of the structures on the Pig Iron Nature Trail in the Elizabeth Furnace Recreation Area in Virginia.*

Higher up the trail, Frémont Crossing at 11,000 feet preserves the very place where General John C. Frémont camped with his expedition in 1842. He had been directed to survey "the rivers and country between the frontiers of Missouri and the base of the Rocky Mountains." He thought he had found the highest peak in the entire chain and determined to scale it. He and five companions set out from camp and worked their way to the summit, climbing the last granite wall in thin moccasins of buffalo skin. On the peak Frémont drove a ramrod into the rock and "unfurled the national flag to wave where never the flag waved before." He named it for himself and though it may not be the highest in the Rockies, Mount Frémont belongs in the fraternity of great mountains.

Such places constitute a resource of high merit in the cultural history and development of America. We can tell what the scene was like during the trappers' age because of the art work of Alfred Jacob Miller. He was the first painter of the upper Rocky Mountains, and the only one to catch the mountain trappers on the spot at the summit of their pride. A Baltimorean and an artist who had studied abroad, he was engaged in 1837 by a celebrated Scottish adventurer, Sir William Drummond Stewart, to join an expedition for the West. He was, so to speak, being assigned as a news photographer to cover an area and an era.

Consequently, he made the first paintings of landmarks on the trail to Oregon: Scotts Bluff, Chimney Rock, the Wind Rivers, the Grand Tetons. He was the artistic chronicler of the mountain men in the age of Jim Bridger, and he painted them from almost every angle—setting traps in stream beds, pitching a lonely camp, hunting buffalo, dancing around a campfire, struggling in the quicksand, meeting the Indians in summer rendezvous on the Green River. His sketches, wash drawings and watercolors brim with spontaneity.

Miller's paintings were long overlooked and forgotten until their rediscovery in 1935 by Mrs. Mae Reed Porter of Kansas City. She knocked on many doors until fate led her to Bernard DeVoto. The result was the publication of many Miller paintings for the first time as illustrations for DeVoto's *Across the Wide Missouri*. Surely it was no coincidence that the late historian, DeVoto, authority on Lewis and Clark, as well as on the trappers, wrote with expertise on the National Forests and made grazing problems a special province of his many-sided life.

Grazing and the National Forests have grown up together through history and art. Charles Russell, "the Cowboy Artist," began his career as a teenage buckaroo in the Montana Territory of the 1880's. He herded stock and painted scenes of life on what is now the Lewis and Clark National Forest in the vicinity of Great Falls. He saw the last days of the open range, the wild buffalo herds and the Indians still untamed and untrammeled. He was not only a cowman but hunter, trapper and squawman, who lived with the Blood Indians. No other important artist understood Western ways so intimately.

Once he began to cultivate his talent, Charlie Russell sensed that he was part of a transition in time. He recorded the West with virtuosity and versatility, using pen and ink, oil, watercolor and bronze sculpture. He painted 50 buffalo hunt scenes—scenes in the dead of winter and in the dust of dry summer—Indian per-

sonalities in all their dignity, wildlife, everything that figured in the patina of his time and place. He would kid himself or his friends, and when he depicted two or three cowboys trying to handle a tough steer, the cowboys usually came off second best. But studies of the equipment they wore were finely detailed.

The popular stories of Zane Grey also are set on lands now within National Forests. Grey was an Easterner from Ohio, but he wrote scores of novels about ranchers, cowhands, miners, gunfighters and lurching stage coaches. During what may be called his "Arizona period" he worked in a little cabin near the town of Payson surrounded by the Tonto National Forest. He was just below the great natural escarpment called the Mogollon Rim, or Tonto Rim, which forms the boundary with the Coconino and Sitgreaves National Forests, and these environs became the setting of his story, "Under the Tonto Rim."

*The "Gates on the Mountains," where the Missouri River is hemmed in by cliffs for seven miles in Helena National Forest, Montana, were named by Lewis and Clark.*

*Green Mountain National Forest: Picturesque covered bridge crosses Madison River at Warren, Vermont.*

From the pine-clad mountains underneath the Mogollon down to the cactus-studded desert near Phoenix, the Tonto National Forest is rich in history and tradition—and mystery. In all America there is only one spot with the aura of the Lost Dutchman Mine. The legend owes its genesis to a German immigrant, Jacob Waltz, commonly known as the "Old Dutchman," who was believed to be working a mine of great mineral wealth—at least on several occasions he arrived in Florence and Phoenix with sackfuls of gold nuggets and murmurings about his hidden mine. On his deathbed in 1891 in Phoenix, Waltz gave vague directions to his mine as part of an old Spanish digging that lay in the Superstition Mountains somewhere in the vicinity of the Weaver's Needle rock formation. Whether fact or fiction, the story of the Lost Dutchman has stimulated an unending search for the treasure.

The Superstition Wilderness, 40 miles from downtown Phoenix, is probably the closest wilderness to any major city in the United States. Each spring the Don's Club, a civic group of Phoenix, conducts a hike into the reddish canyons of the Superstitions, bold landmarks of the desert, which rise abruptly from the desert floor of some 2,000 feet elevation to 6,000 feet. Whether on foot or horse, here it is possible to see wild desert country much the way the Spanish explorers saw it, and as the Apaches knew it before them.

The most notable exploration of them all in the National Forests was made by Lewis and Clark.

Between 1804 and 1806, in President Jefferson's behalf, they traversed more than half a continent, from St. Louis to the Pacific Ocean, conducting the first survey of the resources in the Western United States. (They had invited William Bartram to serve as botanist of the expedition, but he was then aging and ailing and had declined.) With each passing generation their epochal achievement has reached deeper into the national conscience and pride. In 1965, a joint study of Federal, state and local agencies of the Lewis and Clark Expedition culminated in a proposal to commemorate the entire route and to identify the major points of interest. Some ones lie along the 270 miles of their trail that extends through nine National Forests.

*Jefferson National Forest: Abandoned iron furnaces are scattered throughout Forests in East and Midwest.*

*Swans are usually seen near rustic Falling Spring Mill, Mark Twain National Forest.*

*A popular place with tourists is ruins of Pecos Pueblo, Santa Fe National Forest, New Mexico.*

On August 12, 1805, four white men first beheld the western slopes of the Rockies. Captain Meriwether Lewis was one. With three others, he crossed Lemhi Pass—now designated as a National Historical Site—and persuaded the local Shoshone Indians to come back into Montana to help the main party. In what is now the Sacajawea Historial Area of the Salmon National Forest, their guide, Sacajawea, was reunited with her brother, Camehwait. Later the entire party moved up the North Fork of the Salmon River, recrossing the Continental Divide at Lost Trail Pass, dropping down into the Bitterroot Valley to present-day Lolo, Montana. Later they followed the 150-mile Lolo Trail, descending along the river and then the Clearwater River to the point where it joins the Snake at present-day Lewiston, Idaho, then pressing downstream along the Snake and the Columbia before winter set in.

*Hammond Canyon in Manti-La Sal National Forest, Utah, is one indication of area's unusual geology.*

They returned this way in 1806. At Lolo the expedition split into two groups. Lewis led a small party over the Continental Divide at Lewis and Clark Pass, then to the Great Falls of the Missouri to present-day Browning and to Fort Benton, Montana. Clark, meanwhile, had gone south through the Bitterroot Valley, crossing the Continental Divide at Gibbons Pass. His group finally rejoined Lewis and the rest of the "Corps of Discovery" at the confluence of the Yellowstone and Missouri Rivers for the last long leg down the Missouri to St. Louis.

Their descriptions fit the country, even now, with extraordinary accuracy. One century from now, two centuries from now, the lands along their course may be truer to their native form.

Certainly the adventures of Lewis and Clark will fire the imagination of generations to come. In the National Forests that this famous expedition traversed, they may find the reality of dreams of the American past—dreams to live with, and to enhance the American future.

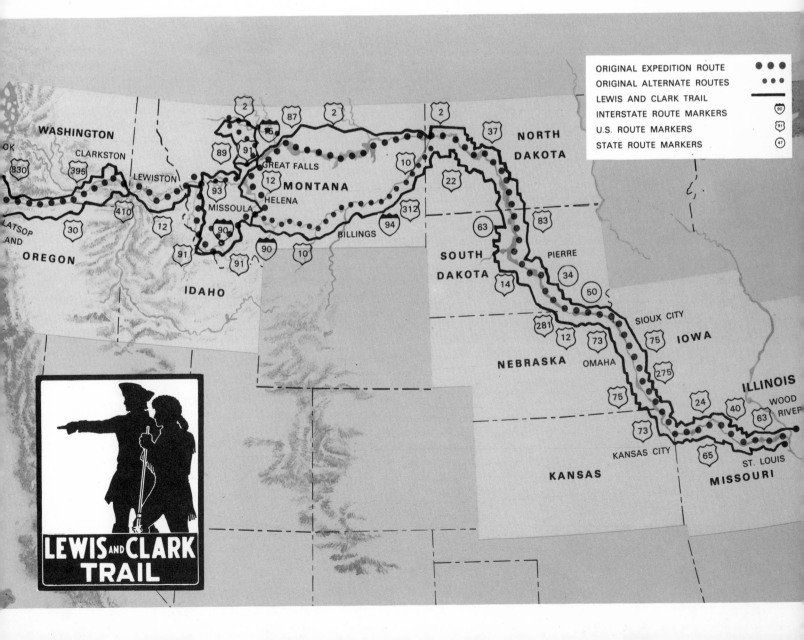

# EPILOGUE

By Edward P. Cliff,
Former Chief, Forest Service

A typical workday in the National Forest System (if, indeed, there is such a day) spans a wide variety of activities and interests in a wide range of places extending virtually the length and breadth of the land.

The sun rises on the typical day on more than four million deer, elk, bighorn sheep, bear and other big-game animals at home in their National Forest habitat. It shines on many millions of small game and other animals in trees, burrows and caves throughout the National Forest System. Countless birds stretch their wings, feed their young and preen themselves in the morning sun.

If our typical day occurs in May, 50 or 60 wildfires are likely to break out and to char about 700 acres before they are detected and extinguished. Lookouts are constantly scanning the horizon, patrol planes are in the air, and, wherever the fire danger is high, Smokejumpers, airtankers and suppression crews are standing by for action.

Thousands of men and women of the Forest Service are involved in many kinds of programs that must proceed at the same time. More than 200 square miles of land are photographed from the air in a day in order to aid in mapmaking and resource management. Forest Service crews and contractors are engaged in maintaining roads and building new roads. They rehabilitate rangeland; improve timber stands and fish and game habitats; construct or reconstruct family camping and picnic units—all their work is directly related to conserving, restoring and enhancing the land for usefulness and beauty. In the course of a year, reforestation projects involve planting or seeding of 250,000 acres. In the course of a day, over 400 acres of deteriorated hillsides and several miles of eroding stream channels are planted in order to improve and stabilize watersheds.

One out of every three acres of the National Forest System is rangeland and by noon the sun is likely to shine on the backs of about six million head of grazing livestock. In many areas, rangers are inspecting the range by jeep or horseback, discussing its management and long range needs with some of the 20,000 permittees.

During the hunting season many thousands of sportsmen are in the National Forests on any given day. By the end of the season, more than 600,000 are likely to hang trophy animals by their camps. Special areas are safeguarded for endangered species, such as the great condors of the Los Padres National Forest in California and the delicate little Kirtland's warblers of Huron National Forest in Michigan.

The warming rays of the sun drive trout, bass and other fish into the depths and shadows along many of the 81,000 miles of streams and rivers and thousands of lakes in the National Forests. And while the fish seek cool, quiet refuge, they in turn are sought for the evening's dinner by as many as half a million men, women and children, armed with fishing rods and high hope.

On a summer day, those fishermen are part of more than two million Americans engaged in camping, picnicking, hiking, studying nature, picture-taking or other vacation pursuits. In a year's time, we expect about 150 million twelve-hour visitor-days to be spent in recreation —and that volume is rising.

While the public finds the National Forests a source of healthful leisure, the timber industry considers many of these woodlands a vital workshop. Between breakfast and supper time, powersaws and logging trucks harvest more than 50 million board feet of National Forest timber, which is removed in accordance with sound forestry practices and detailed plans. For the right to remove this timber, enough to build 5,000 houses, some 25,000 operators, large and small, will pay about $800,000 into the Federal Treasury on that typical day.

All these activities are conducted under the principle of multiple use, a concept that is adapted both to the immediate needs of people and the long-range needs of resources and the nation. While in particular areas one or more uses may be primary, over large areas no use is ruled out. In a broad sense, the principle encompasses the pleasures of fishing, the protection of wilderness, the practical production of timber, beef and wool, the financial return to the treasury of revenue from commercial users, the benefits of protected watersheds, the economic strength of rural areas and the natural beauty of the nation.

Thus, the National Forest System reflects the best qualities of people themselves. The people are part of the National Forests. We administer the lands in the people's behalf, in cooperation and collaboration with the people every day of the year. For example, on one hand, millions of board feet of National Forest timber could not be harvested on a working day without the help of the far-flung timber industry. On the other hand, cooperating state and private agencies made possible the development of the Kirtland's Warbler Management Area in Michigan. Their research and determined efforts provided information and support which allowed the Forest Service to strengthen its management plans. Every working day provides new illustrations of the close ties between the American people and their National Forest System.

This attractive book has recounted the past, reported the present, and forecast the future. It opens the door to appreciation of the National Forests. For full understanding and enjoyment, we invite Americans to explore the treasures that are theirs.

*Edward P. Cliff, Former Chief, United States Forest Service: Among his distinguished predecessors is Gifford Pinchot, who became head of Forestry Division in 1898.*

173

# BASIC
# NATIONAL FOREST
# INFORMATION
## Part 1
## Complete List of National Forests

### Alabama

William B. Bankhead National Forest (178,739 acres). Headquarters: Montgomery, Ala.

Conecuh National Forest (83,900 acres). Headquarters: Montgomery, Ala.

Talladega National Forest (357,470 acres). Headquarters: Montgomery, Ala.

Tuskegee National Forest (10,778 acres). Headquarters: Montgomery, Ala.

### Alaska

Chugach National Forest (4,723,397 acres). Headquarters: Anchorage, Alaska.

Tongass National Forest (16,011,643 acres). Headquarters: Juneau, Alaska, and Ketchikan, Alaska.

### Arizona

Apache National Forest (1,806,751 acres)—partly in New Mexico. Headquarters: Springerville, Ariz.

Coconino National Forest (1,808,043 acres). Headquarters: Flagstaff, Ariz.

Coronado National Forest (1,791,114 acres)—partly in New Mexico. Headquarters: Tucson, Ariz.

Kaibab National Forest (1,727,995 acres). Headquarters: Williams, Ariz.

Prescott National Forest (1,247,834 acres). Headquarters: Prescott, Ariz.

Sitgreaves National Forest (795,504 acres). Headquarters: Holbrook, Ariz.

Tonto National Forest (2,890,853 acres). Headquarters: Phoenix, Ariz.

### Arkansas

Ouachita National Forest (1,563,383 acres)—partly in Oklahoma. Headquarters: Hot Springs, Ark.

Ozark National Forest (1,088,164 acres). Headquarters: Russellville, Ark.

St. Francis National Forest (20,611 acres). Headquarters: Russellville, Ark.

### California

Angeles National Forest (648,866 acres). Headquarters: Pasadena, Calif.

Calaveras Bigtree (379 acres). Headquarters: Sonora, Calif.

Cleveland National Forest (393,085 acres). Headquarters: San Diego, Calif.

Eldorado National Forest (652,527 acres). Headquarters: Placerville, Calif.

Inyo National Forest (1,835,960 acres)—partly in Nevada. Headquarters: Bishop, Calif.

Klamath National Forest (1,696,965 acres)—partly in Oregon. Headquarters: Yreka, Calif.

Lassen National Forest (1,045,624 acres). Headquarters: Susanville, Calif.

Los Padres National Forest (1,724,108 acres). Headquarters: Santa Barbara, Calif.

Mendocino National Forest (872,237 acres). Headquarters: Willows, Calif.

Modoc National Forest (1,689,508 acres). Headquarters: Alturas, Calif.

Plumas National Forest (1,146,732 acres). Headquarters: Quincy, Calif.

San Bernardino National Forest (616,315 acres). Headquarters: San Bernardino, Calif.

Sequoia National Forest (1,115,858 acres). Headquarters: Porterville, Calif.

Shasta National Forest (1,003,265 acres). Headquarters: Redding, Calif.

Sierra National Forest (1,293,180 acres). Headquarters: Fresno, Calif.

Six Rivers National Forest (939,399 acres). Headquarters: Eureka, Calif.

Stanislaus National Forest (896,312 acres). Headquarters: Sonora, Calif.

Tahoe National Forest (696,777 acres). Headquarters: Nevada City, Calif.

Trinity National Forest (1,062,989 acres). Headquarters: Redding, Calif.

*View of majestic Mount Hood (11,245 feet), the highest point in Oregon, with bear grass in foreground.*

## Colorado

Arapaho National Forest (1,003,873 acres). Headquarters: Golden, Colo.

Grand Mesa National Forest (360,964 acres). Headquarters: Delta, Colo.

Gunnison National Forest (1,662,860 acres). Headquarters: Gunnison, Colo.

Pike National Forest (1,106,101 acres). Headquarters: Colorado Springs, Colo.

Rio Grande National Forest (1,799,389 acres). Headquarters: Monte Vista, Colo.

Roosevelt National Forest (776,139 acres). Headquarters: Fort Collins, Colo.

Routt National Forest (1,125,045 acres). Headquarters: Steamboat Springs, Colo.

San Isabel National Forest (1,106,510 acres). Headquarters: Pueblo, Colo.

San Juan National Forest (1,850,405 acres). Headquarters: Durango, Colo.

Uncompahgre National Forest (957,004 acres). Headquarters: Delta, Colo.

White River National Forest (1,160,183 acres). Headquarters: Glenwood Springs, Colo.

## Florida

Apalachicola National Forest (556,972 acres). Headquarters: Tallahassee, Fla.

Ocala National Forest (361,497 acres). Headquarters: Tallahassee, Fla.

Osceola National Forest (157,233 acres). Headquarters: Tallahassee, Fla.

## Georgia

Chattahoochee National Forest (680,618 acres). Headquarters: Gainesville, Ga.

Oconee National Forest (102,911 acres). Headquarters: Gainesville, Ga.

## Idaho

Boise National Forest (2,632,321 acres). Headquarters: Boise, Idaho.

Caribou National Forest (978,255 acres)—partly in Utah and Wyoming. Headquarters: Pocatello, Idaho.

Challis National Forest (2,447,243 acres). Headquarters: Challis, Idaho.

Clearwater National Forest (1,675,562 acres). Headquarters: Orofino, Idaho.

Coeur d'Alene National Forest (723,168 acres). Headquarters: Coeur d'Alene, Idaho.

Kaniksu National Forest (1,621,898 acres)—partly in Montana and Washington. Headquarters: Sandpoint, Idaho.

Nezperce National Forest (2,198,094 acres). Headquarters: Grangeville, Idaho.

Payette National Forest (2,307,158 acres). Headquarters: McCall, Idaho.

Salmon National Forest (1,767,585 acres). Headquarters: Salmon, Idaho.

St. Joe National Forest (862,018 acres). Headquarters: St. Maries, Idaho.

Sawtooth National Forest (1,731,526 acres)—partly in Utah. Headquarters: Twin Falls, Idaho.

Targhee National Forest (1,663,363 acres)—partly in Wyoming. Headquarters: St. Anthony, Idaho.

## Illinois

Shawnee National Forest (217,982 acres). Headquarters: Harrisburg, Ill.

## Indiana

Hoosier National Forest (134,779 acres). Headquarters: Bedford, Ind.

## Kentucky

Daniel Boone National Forest (464,683 acres). Headquarters: Winchester, Ky.

## Louisiana

Kisatchie National Forest (593,064 acres). Headquarters: Alexandria, La.

## Michigan

Huron National Forest (415,493 acres). Headquarters: Cadillac, Mich.

Manistee National Forest (465,140 acres). Headquarters: Cadillac, Mich.

Ottawa National Forest (886,484 acres). Headquarters: Ironwood, Mich.

Hiawatha National Forests (839,960 acres)—two national forests. Headquarters: Escanaba, Mich.

## Minnesota

Chippewa National Forest (644,602 acres). Headquarters: Cass Lake, Minn.

Superior National Forest (2,040,569 acres). Headquarters: Duluth, Minn.

## Mississippi

Bienville National Forest (175,697 acres). Headquarters: Jackson, Miss.

Delta National Forest (58,923 acres). Headquarters: Jackson, Miss.

DeSoto National Forest (501,548 acres). Headquarters: Jackson, Miss.

Holly Springs National Forest (143,729 acres). Headquarters: Jackson, Miss.

Homochitto National Forest (189,053 acres). Headquarters: Jackson, Miss.

Tombigbee National Forest (65,254 acres). Headquarters: Jackson, Miss.

## Missouri

Clark National Forest (768,254 acres). Headquarters: Rolla, Mo.

Mark Twain National Forest (608,719 acres). Headquarters: Springfield, Mo.

## Montana

Beaverhead National Forest (2,111,070 acres). Headquarters: Dillon, Mont.

Bitterroot National Forest (1,575,919 acres)—partly in Idaho. Headquarters: Hamilton, Mont.

Custer National Forest (1,185,663 acres)—partly in South Dakota. Headquarters: Billings, Mont.

Deerlodge National Forest (1,181,276 acres). Headquarters: Butte, Mont.

Flathead National Forest (2,341,664 acres). Headquarters: Kalispell, Mont.

Gallatin National Forest (1,701,338 acres). Headquarters: Bozeman, Mont.

Helena National Forest (969,000 acres). Headquarters: Helena, Mont.

Kootenai National Forest (1,819,545 acres)—partly in Idaho. Headquarters: Libby, Mont.

Lewis and Clark National Forest (1,834,612 acres). Headquarters: Great Falls, Mont.

Lolo National Forest (2,086,234 acres). Headquarters: Missoula, Mont.

## Nebraska

Nebraska National Forest (245,414 acres). Headquarters: Lincoln, Nebr.

## Nevada

Humboldt National Forest (2,512,258 acres). Headquarters: Elko, Nev.

Toiyabe National Forest (3,119,593 acres)—partly in California. Headquarters: Reno, Nev.

## New Hampshire

White Mountain National Forest (716,157 acres)—partly in Maine. Headquarters: Laconia, N. H.

## New Mexico

Carson National Forest (1,419,732 acres). Headquarters: Taos, N. Mex.

Cibola National Forest (1,599,337 acres). Headquarters: Albuquerque, N. Mex.

Gila National Forest (2,694,447 acres). Headquarters: Silver City, N. Mex.

Lincoln National Forest (1,085,302 acres). Headquarters: Alamogordo, N. Mex.

Santa Fe National Forest (1,440,511 acres). Headquarters: Santa Fe, N. Mex.

## North Carolina

Croatan National Forest (152,373 acres). Headquarters: Asheville, N. C.

Nantahala National Forest (449,281 acres). Headquarters: Asheville, N. C.

Pisgah National Forest (478,927 acres). Headquarters: Asheville, N. C.

Uwharrie National Forest (43,571 acres). Headquarters: Asheville, N. C.

## Ohio

Wayne National Forest (118,944 acres). Headquarters: Bedford, Indiana.

## Oregon

Deschutes National Forest (1,587,690 acres). Headquarters: Bend, Oreg.

Fremont National Forest (1,208,302 acres). Headquarters: Lakeview, Oreg.

Malheur National Forest (1,204,974 acres). Headquarters: John Day, Oreg.

Mount Hood National Forest (1,115,746 acres). Headquarters: Portland, Oreg.

Ochoco National Forest (845,855 acres). Headquarters: Prineville, Oreg.

Rogue River National Forest (621,473 acres)—partly in California. Headquarters: Medford, Oreg.

Siskiyou National Forest (1,081,006 acres)—partly in California. Headquarters: Grants Pass, Oreg.

Siuslaw National Forest (618,685 acres). Headquarters: Corvallis, Oreg.

Umatilla National Forest (1,389,709 acres)—partly in Washington. Headquarters: Pendleton, Oreg.

Umpqua National Forest (984,497 acres). Headquarters: Roseburg, Oreg.

Wallowa National Forest (981,084 acres). Headquarters: Baker, Oreg.

Whitman National Forest (1,516,010 acres). Headquarters: Baker, Oreg.

Willamette National Forest (1,665,979 acres). Headquarters: Eugene, Oreg.

Winema National Forest (908,984 acres). Headquarters: Klamath Falls, Oreg.

## Pennsylvania

Allegheny National Forest (475,749 acres). Headquarters: Warren, Pa.

## Puerto Rico

Caribbean National Forest (27,889 acres). Headquarters: Rio Piedras, Puerto Rico.

## South Carolina

Francis Marion National Forest (245,657 acres). Headquarters: Columbia, S. C.

Sumter National Forest (342,082 acres). Headquarters: Columbia, S. C.

## South Dakota

Black Hills National Forest (1,221,411 acres)—partly in Wyoming. Headquarters: Custer, S. Dak.

## Tennessee

Cherokee National Forest (600,764 acres). Headquarters: Cleveland, Tenn.

## Texas

Angelina National Forest (154,389 acres). Headquarters: Lufkin, Texas.

Davy Crockett National Forest (161,556 acres). Headquarters: Lufkin, Texas.

Sabine National Forest (183,843 acres). Headquarters: Lufkin, Texas.

Sam Houston National Forest (158,235 acres). Headquarters: Lufkin, Texas.

## Utah

Ashley National Forest (1,271,146 acres). Headquarters: Vernal, Utah.

Cache National Forest (673,035 acres)—partly in Idaho. Headquarters: Logan, Utah.

Dixie National Forest (1,883,688 acres). Headquarters: Cedar City, Utah.

Fishlake National Forest (1,424,538 acres). Headquarters: Richfield, Utah.

Manti-La Sal National Forest (1,236,368 acres)—partly in Colorado. Headquarters: Price, Utah.

Uinta National Forest (794,686 acres). Headquarters: Provo, Utah.

Wasatch National Forest (876,820 acres)—partly in Wyoming. Headquarters: Salt Lake City, Utah.

## Vermont

Green Mountain National Forest (233,463 acres). Headquarters: Rutland, Vt.

*The Cheat River in Monongahela National Forest, which was established in 1920.*

### Virginia

George Washington National Forest (1,018,021 acres)—partly in West Virginia. Headquarters: Harrisonburg, Va.

Jefferson National Forest (565,828 acres). Headquarters: Roanoke, Va.

### Washington

Colville National Forest (939,919 acres). Headquarters: Colville, Wash.

Gifford Pinchot National Forest (1,259,910 acres). Headquarters: Vancouver, Wash.

Mount Baker National Forest (1,818,182 acres). Headquarters: Bellingham, Wash.

Okanogan National Forest (1,520,448 acres). Headquarters: Okanogan, Wash.

Olympic National Forest (621,756 acres). Headquarters: Olympia, Wash.

Snoqualmie National Forest (1,211,901 acres). Headquarters: Seattle, Wash.

Wenatchee National Forest (1,731,076 acres). Headquarters: Wenatchee, Wash.

### West Virginia

Monongahela National Forest (808,898 acres). Headquarters: Elkins, W. Va.

### Wisconsin

Chequamegon National Forest (831,327 acres). Headquarters: Park Falls, Wis.

Nicolet National Forest (643,875 acres). Headquarters: Rhinelander, Wis.

### Wyoming

Bighorn National Forest (1,113,769 acres). Headquarters: Sheridan, Wyo.

Bridger National Forest (1,700,029 acres). Headquarters: Kemmerer, Wyo.

Medicine Bow National Forest (1,094,824 acres). Headquarters: Laramie, Wyo.

Shoshone National Forest (2,424,937 acres). Headquarters: Cody, Wyo.

Teton National Forest (1,700,820 acres). Headquarters: Jackson, Wyo.

# Part 2

# National Forest Units of the

# National Wilderness Preservation System

## Arizona

**Chiricahua Wilderness,** 18,000 acres of the Coronado National Forest (headquarters: Tucson). On the crest of the Chiricahua Range with precipitous scenic canyons radiating from the summit. Among game species is the rare Chiricahua squirrel, found only in this vicinity.

**Galiuro Wilderness,** 52,717 acres of the Coronado National Forest (headquarters: Tucson). Knifelike mountains jutting out of the Arizona plain. Extremely steep slopes limit travel to constructed trails. Good hunting for experienced travelers.

**Mazatzal Wilderness,** 205,137 acres of the Tonto National Forest (headquarters: Phoenix). Precipitous topography containing many geological formations. Wildlife, but no fishing.

**Sierra Ancha Wilderness,** 20,850 acres of the Tonto National Forest (headquarters: Phoenix). Precipitous mountains. Prehistoric and Pueblo Indian cliff dwellings. Varied vegetation and wildlife.

**Superstition Wilderness,** 124,117 acres of the Tonto National Forest (headquarters: Phoenix). Extremely rough with occasional prominent peaks. Abounds with mining folklore of the Southwest of the prospecting days. Walking tour sponsored every spring by the Dons Club of Phoenix.

## California

**Caribou Wilderness,** 19,080 acres of the Lassen National Forest (headquarters: Susanville). A mountainous area of volcanic origin near Mt. Lassen in northern California. Attractive small lakes with good fishing and some wildlife.

**Cucamonga Wilderness,** 9,022 acres of the San Bernardino National Forest (headquarters: San Bernardino). Gentle to rugged topography reaching maximum altitude of 8,911 feet. Habitat of deer and mountain sheep. Challenging to hikers, with rewards of exceptional views.

**Dome Land Wilderness,** 62,121 acres of the Sequoia National Forest (headquarters: Porterville). Picturesque domes and spires of bare rock. Elevations from 3,000 to 9,529 feet. Traversed by the precipitous South Fork of Kern River Canyon. Virgin forests cover 6,000 acres.

**Hoover Wilderness,** 8,979 acres of the Inyo National Forest (headquarters: Bishop), and 33,800 acres of the Toiyabe National Forest (headquarters: Reno, Nevada). Rugged canyons and jagged peaks approaching 13,000 feet. Mountain lakes and cascading streams. Meadows carpeted with spring flowers. Abundant wildlife, fishing and remnants of five glaciers.

NATIONAL FOREST UNITS
OF THE
NATIONAL WILDERNESS
PRESERVATION SYSTEM

**John Muir Wilderness**, 228,932 acres of the Inyo National Forest (headquarters: Bishop), and 274,246 acres of the Sierra National Forest (headquarters: Fresno). Spectacular Sierra Crest country with elevations up to nearly 14,500 feet at Mount Whitney. Hundreds of lakes and streams, many with native golden trout. John Muir Trail traverses much of the area. Wildlife, vegetation and geologic features in abundance.

**Marble Mountain Wilderness**, 213,363 acres of the Klamath National Forest (headquarters: Yreka). Outstanding mountain scenery of two types: the Marble Mountains of white and grey marble, and high granitic peaks to the south. A wide variety of tree species. Both stream and lake fishing.

**Minarets Wilderness**, 61,433 acres of the Inyo National Forest (headquarters: Bishop), and 48,051 acres of the Sierra National Forest (headquarters: Fresno). Rugged peaks and spires of unusual grandeur. One of the finest climbing regions in the Sierra Nevada. Many streams, nearly 400 lakes, and about 25 remnants of glaciers.

**Mokelumne Wilderness**, 41,560 acres of the Eldorado National Forest (headquarters: Placerville), and 8,840 acres of the Stanislaus National Forest (headquarters: Sonora). High granite crest zone. Rugged and sparsely timbered. Abundant wildlife. Lake and stream fishing.

**San Gorgonio Wilderness**, 34,644 acres of the San Bernardino National Forest (headquarters: San Bernardino). San Gorgonio Peak, 11,485 feet; desert to alpine scenery and vegetation.

**San Jacinto Wilderness**, 20,564 acres of the San Bernardino National Forest (headquarters: San Bernardino). Mountains, meadows, and flats atop precipitous cliffs rising high above the Palm Springs desert country.

**San Rafael Wilderness**, 142,722 acres of the Los Padres National Forest (headquarters: Santa Barbara). It embraces the main range of the San Rafael Mountains, running uniquely east-west, and the headwaters of the Sisquoc River. Vegetation is mostly brush and chaparral. On the ridges, grassy meadows, or potreros, were campsites of the Chumash Indians, who left pictographs and abalone-shell jewelry as vestiges of their culture. The Sisquoc Condor Sanctuary is in the heart of the San Rafael. This is the first former primitive area added by Congress to the National Wilderness Preservation System; President Lyndon B. Johnson signed the law for establishment of the Wilderness on March 21, 1968.

**South Warner Wilderness**, 68,507 acres of the Modoc National Forest (headquarters: Alturas). A 15-mile-long ridge, most of it over 9,000 feet in elevation. Numerous peaks, small meadows, and lakes. Summer range for mule deer.

**Thousand Lakes Wilderness**, 15,695 acres of the Lassen National Forest (headquarters: Susanville). Of particular interest because of volcanic-origin peaks, and lava flows. It has several timber-bound fishing lakes, and peaks of scenic grandeur.

**Yolla-Bolly-Middle Eel Wilderness**, 72,316 acres of the Mendocino National Forest (headquarters: Willows), and 36,135 acres of the Shasta-Trinity National Forests (headquarters: Redding). Variety of natural rugged scenery. Abundant wildlife. Good stream fishing in early part of season.

## Colorado

**La Garita Wilderness**, 24,322 acres of the Gunnison National Forest (headquarters: Gunnison), and 22,700 acres of the Rio Grande National Forest (headquarters: Monte Vista). Along the Continental Divide with peaks exceeding 14,000 feet. Abundance of wildlife in alpine and subalpine settings. Fishing in streams and lakes.

**Maroon Bells-Snowmass Wilderness**, 71,060 acres of the White River National Forest (headquarters: Glenwood Springs). Includes Snowmass Mountain, Maroon Bells and Pyramid Peak, all over 14,000 feet. Mountain sheep summer and winter at Conundrum Hot Springs. Excellent fishing.

**Mt. Zirkel Wilderness**, 72,472 acres of the Routt National Forest (headquarters: Steamboat Springs). High, rough, scenic country astride the Continental Divide. Mt. Zirkel, 12,220 feet, is the highest peak. Many lakes and streams with good fishing. An elk summer range.

**Rawah Wilderness**, 26,674 acres of the Roosevelt National Forest (headquarters Fort Collins). In Medicine Bow Range. Includes a small glacier and numerous glacial lakes. Part of area is exceptionally rugged. Good fishing.

**West Elk Wilderness**, 62,000 acres of the Gunnison National Forest (headquarters: Gunnison). Embraces portions of several high mountain ranges, open park ranges, lakes and rushing streams. Summer range of many deer and elk.

## Idaho

**Selway-Bitterroot Wilderness** (also partly in Montana), 164,946 acres of the Bitterroot National Forest (headquarters: Hamilton, Montana), 265,580 acres of the Clearwater National Forest (headquarters: Orofino), and 588,129 acres of the Nezperce National Forest (headquarters: Grangeville). Mountainous, wooded area lying mostly west of the Bitterroot Range. Wildlife and vegetation of great variety.

## Minnesota

**Boundary Waters Canoe Area**, 747,099 acres of the Superior National Forest (headquarters: Duluth). It adjoins Quetico Provincial Park in Ontario for almost a hundred miles along the United States-Canadian border and constitutes the finest canoe country in America with hundreds of lakes and streams. Excellent fishing in more remote regions. This is the largest wilderness east of the Rockies.

## Montana

**Anaconda-Pintlar Wilderness**, 72,526 acres of the Beaverhead National Forest (headquarters: Dillon), 44,115 acres of the Deerlodge National Forest (headquarters: Butte), and 41,162 acres of the Bitterroot National Forest (headquarters: Hamilton). A scenic chain of high, barren, and precipitous peaks along the Continental Divide. Forested slopes flank the crest. Numerous lakes and streams.

**Bob Marshall Wilderness**, 710,000 acres of the Flathead National Forest (headquarters: Kalispell), and 240,000 acres of the Lewis and Clark National Forest (headquarters: Great Falls). A spectacular mountain area with a wide variety of flora and fauna. Outstanding opportunities for elk hunting and cutthroat trout fishing. Of great geologic interest, climaxed by the "Chinese Wall."

**Cabinet Mountains Wilderness** (also partly in Idaho), 39,663 acres of the Kaniksu National Forest (headquarters: Sandpoint, Idaho), and 54,609 acres of the Kootenai National Forest (headquarters: Libby). A lofty, peak-studded area of scenic grandeur. Big game and wild flowers in abundance.

**Gates of the Mountains Wilderness**, 28,562 acres of the Helena National Forest (headquarters: Helena). Spectacular limestone cliffs and other geologic formations. The name "Gates of the Mountains" was given by Lewis and Clark after they had viewed the deep gorge cut by the Missouri River.

**Selway-Bitterroot Wilderness** (also partly in Idaho), 244,150 acres of the Bitterroot National Forest (headquarters: Hamilton), and 7,780 acres of the Lolo National Forest (headquarters: Missoula). Mountainous, wooded area lying mostly west of the Bitterroot Range. Wildlife and vegetation of great variety.

## Nevada

**Jarbidge Wilderness**, 64,667 acres of the Humboldt National Forest (headquarters: Elko). Rugged mountainous terrain with eight peaks over 10,000 feet. Deer are plentiful, small game and birds numerous, fishing good. This is one of the most scenic remote spots in Nevada.

## New Hampshire

**Great Gulf Wilderness,** 5,552 acres of the White Mountain National Forest (headquarters: Laconia). A rough, rugged mountain basin on the slopes of Mount Washington. Accessible by trail. Elevations from 1,700 to 5,800 feet.

## New Mexico

**Gila Wilderness** (partially reclassified in 1953, balance awaiting review), 433,690 acres of the Gila National Forest (headquarters: Silver City). Topography rough to precipitous. Many deep box canyons. Good hunting and trout fishing.

**Pecos Wilderness,** 25,357 acres of the Carson National Forest (headquarters: Taos), and 142,059 acres of the Santa Fe National Forest (headquarters: Santa Fe). High back country with trout lakes and streams; elk and deer hunting.

**San Pedro Parks Wilderness,** 41,132 acres of the Santa Fe National Forest (headquarters: Santa Fe). A high mountain plateau. Dense stands of spruce and open meadows with small trout streams. Some deer, turkey and grouse hunting.

**Wheeler Peak Wilderness,** 6,027 acres of the Carson National Forest (headquarters: Taos). Outstanding scenery—includes Wheeler Peak, elevation 13,160 feet, highest in New Mexico.

**White Mountain Wilderness,** 31,171 acres of the Lincoln National Forest (headquarters: Alamogordo). A variety of mountain vistas and forest flora. Elevation 6,000 to 11,000 feet.

## North Carolina

**Linville Gorge Wilderness,** 7,575 acres of the Pisgah National Forest (headquarters: Asheville). Deep, rough gorge with cascades, virgin timber and flowering shrubs. Elevation from 1,000 to 4,000 feet.

**Shining Rock Wilderness,** 13,400 acres of the Pisgah National Forest (headquarters: Asheville). Unique vegetation cover surmounted by Shining Rock Mountain of white quartz. Many waterfalls and springs. Outstanding deer and bear population. Good stream fishing.

## Oregon

**Diamond Peak Wilderness,** 19,240 acres of the Deschutes National Forest (headquarters: Bend), and 16,200 acres of the Willamette National Forest (headquarters: Eugene). Straddles the summit of the Cascade Mountains. Includes snow-capped Diamond Peak, 8,750 feet elevation, and 33 lakes with occasional small mountain meadows adjacent to the lakes.

**Eagle Cap Wilderness,** 220,416 acres of the Wallowa-Whitman National Forests (headquarters: Baker). Embraces some of the highest peaks and best fishing waters in eastern Oregon. Many geological formations. Elk, deer, bear and lesser wildlife species are common.

**Gearhart Mountain Wilderness,** 18,709 acres of the Fremont National Forest (headquarters: Lakeview). Spectacular "Gearhart Notch," rock palisades, good hunting and fishing. Has areas of all local timber types on its slopes.

**Kalmiopsis Wilderness,** 76,900 acres of the Siskiyou National Forest (headquarters: Grants Pass). A rough, steep, mountainous area from 500 to 5,000 feet in elevation. Noted for rare and unusual plants and trees, including rhododendron-like **Kalmiopsis leachiana** and 17 species of conifers. Abundant wildlife and good fishing.

**Mountain Lakes Wilderness,** 23,071 acres of the Winema National Forest (headquarters: Klamath Falls). Mountain lakes within a bowl formed by eight prominent peaks. Elevations range from 5,000 to 7,950 feet. Abundant wildlife and good fishing.

**Mount Hood Wilderness,** 14,160 acres of the Mount Hood National Forest (headquarters: Portland). Occupies the high country north and west of the summit of Mt. Hood. Outstanding examples of alpine meadows and living glaciers surround the peak.

**Mount Washington Wilderness,** 8,625 acres of the Deschutes National Forest (headquarters: Bend), and 38,030 acres of the Willamette National Forest (headquarters: Eugene). Straddles the summit of the Cascade Mountains. Includes snow-capped Mount Washington, Little Belknap and Belknap Craters; vast fields of lava beds of recent origin, open glades and varied alpine trees.

**Strawberry Mountain Wilderness,** 33,003 acres of the Malheur National Forest (headquarters: John Day). Centered around Strawberry Mountain and Strawberry Lake. Occupies the most rugged area in John Day country. High mountain lakes, alpine meadows, unique rock formations and varied tree species.

**Three Sisters Wilderness,** 59,875 acres of the Deschutes National Forest (headquarters: Bend), and 136,833 acres of the Willamette National Forest (headquarters: Eugene). Includes the Three Sisters Mountains; numerous peaks and glaciers, among them Collier Glacier, Oregon's largest, on North Sister. This wilderness contains 111 lakes.

## Washington

**Glacier Peak Wilderness,** 214,759 acres of the Mount Baker National Forest (headquarters: Bellingham), and 236,739 acres of the Wenatchee National Forest (headquarters: Wenatchee). Outstanding for its many glaciers, numerous lakes and alpine scenery. Glacier Peak is the central attraction. More than 30 peaks rise up to 8,000 feet above intervening valleys.

**Goat Rocks Wilderness,** 59,740 acres of the Gifford Pinchot National Forest (headquarters: Vancouver), and 22,940 acres of the Snoqualmie National Forest (headquarters: Seattle). Extremely precipitous peaks, glaciers, several large lakes and great profusion of mountain flora. Mountain goats abundant.

**Mount Adams Wilderness,** 42,411 acres of the Gifford Pinchot National Forest (headquarters: Vancouver). Largely above timberline; spectacular "Around the Mountain" trail.

## Wyoming

**Bridger Wilderness,** 383,300 acres of the Bridger National Forest (headquarters: Kemmerer). In the historic Wind River Range. Elevations from 8,500 to 13,785 feet on Gannett Peak, the highest in Wyoming. Area characterized by massive granite out-crops. Hundreds of lakes and picturesque streams provide excellent fishing. Noted for mountain climbing, pack trips and big game.

**North Absaroka Wilderness,** 351,104 acres of the Shoshone National Forest (headquarters: Cody). Includes glaciers, natural bridge, standing petrified trees. Excellent hunting and fishing.

**South Absaroka Wilderness,** 483,130 acres of the Shoshone National Forest (headquarters: Cody). Fishhawk Glacier; deep, straight-walled canyons, back-country pack horse trips.

**Teton Wilderness,** 563,500 acres of the Teton National Forest (headquarters: Jackson). Region of high plateaus, large valleys and mountain meadows that can be easily traversed. Includes Two Ocean Pass, where Two Ocean Creek divides and sends one stream to the Pacific and one to the Atlantic. Noted for elk hunting and fishing. Summer range for Jackson Hole elk herd.

# Part 3

# Areas Under Review for the
# National Wilderness Preservation System

## (Presently classified as Primitive Areas)

## Arizona

**Blue Range** (also partly in New Mexico), 180,139 acres of the Apache National Forest (headquarters: Springerville). Traversed by the Mogollon Rim with spruce and fir in the high country above the Rim and ponderosa pine in the broken country below. Big game is abundant.

**Mount Baldy,** 7,106 acres of the Apache National Forest (headquarters: Springerville). On northeast slope of Mount Baldy at the head of the West Fork of Little Colorado River. Elevation to 11,496 feet.

**Pine Mountain,** 8,803 acres of the Prescott National Forest (headquarters: Prescott), and 7,596 acres of the Tonto National Forest (headquarters: Phoenix). Moderately rough terrain along Verde Rim. Big game hunting good but difficult because of heavy cover and steep canyons.

**Sycamore Canyon,** 21,496 acres of the Coconino National Forest (headquarters: Flagstaff), 7,638 acres of the Kaibab National Forest (headquarters: Williams), and 20,441 acres of the Prescott National Forest (headquarters: Prescott). Includes a representation of the various canyon types of flora and fauna of northern Arizona. Spectacular geological formations.

## California

**Agua Tibia,** 25,995 acres of the Cleveland National Forest (headquarters: San Diego). California's southernmost classified area. It contains unusual unburned virgin brush flora.

**Desolation Valley,** 41,343 acres of the Eldorado National Forest (headquarters: Placerville). Extremely rough, rugged and alpine in every respect. Elevations from 6,500 to 10,020.

**Devil Canyon-Bear Canyon,** 34,807 acres of the Angeles National Forest (headquarters: Pasadena). Area of deep canyons only 40 miles by road from Los Angeles.

**Emigrant Basin,** 97,020 acres of the Stanislaus National Forest (headquarters: Stanislaus). Includes many lakes, fine fishing and high granite topography.

**High Sierra,** 7,040 acres of the Sequoia National Forest (headquarters: Porterville), and 3,207 acres of the Sierra National Forest (headquarters: Fresno). This extremely rough mountainous area includes magnificent Tehipite Valley. A great variety of vegetation and life zones occur between the valley floor and surrounding heights. Monarch Divide is an area of rugged terrain with few travel routes.

**Salmon Trinity Alps,** 28,576 acres of the Klamath National Forest (headquarters: Yreka), and 194,764 acres of the Shasta-Trinity National Forests (headquarters: Redding). A region of scenic beauty, including granite peaks, many alpine lakes, and numerous streams teeming with trout.

**San Rafael,** 74,458 acres of the Los Padres National Forest (headquarters: Santa Barbara). Embraces main range of San Rafael Mountains.

**Ventana,** 52,769 acres of the Los Padres National Forest (headquarters: Santa Barbara). Area of low elevation but rugged terrain.

## Colorado

**Flat Tops,** 102,124 acres of the White River National Forest (headquarters: Glenwood Springs). Rolling, rim-rocked plateau dotted with ponds. Summer range for the noted White River migratory deer and elk herds.

**Gore Range-Eagle Nest,** 32,379 acres of the Arapaho National Forest (headquarters: Golden), and 28,825 acres of the White River National Forest (headquarters: Glenwood Springs). Spectacular knife ridges and pinnacles of the Gore Range are superlative rock-climbing terrain.

**San Juan,** 238,407 acres of the San Juan National Forest (headquarters: Durango). The Needle Mountains challenge rock climbers from across the nation. The San Juans abound in wildlife. Includes a Grizzly Bear Management Area. Large expanses without trails.

**Uncompahgre,** 53,252 acres of the Uncompahgre National Forest (headquarters: Delta). Extremely rugged mountains, lakes, and waterfalls. Wildlife is varied and abundant.

**Upper Rio Grande,** 56,600 acres of the Rio Grande National Forest (headquarters: Monte Vista). Adjoins the San Juan Primitive Area along the Continental Divide at the headwaters of the Rio Grande. Noted for trout fishing.

**Wilson Mountains,** 9,600 acres of the San Juan National Forest (headquarters: Durango), and 17,747 acres of the Uncompahgre National Forest (headquarters: Delta). Includes five mountains and two major peaks of the Wilson Range. Large and small game are found in considerable numbers.

## Idaho

**Idaho,** 223,996 acres of the Boise National Forest (headquarters: Boise), 74,339 acres of the Challis National Forest (headquarters: Challis), 685,336 acres of the Payette National Forest (headquarters: McCall), and 241,062 acres of the Salmon National Forest (headquarters: Salmon). Rugged, scenic and mountainous, with towering peaks and deep canyons. Embraces the Middle Fork of Salmon River, noted for float boating and fishing. Excellent hunting, with large herds of deer and elk. Bighorn sheep are common along the river.

**Salmon River Breaks,** 122,500 acres of the Bitterroot National Forest (headquarters: Hamilton, Mont.), and 94,370 acres of the Nezperce National Forest (headquarters: Grangeville). Good hunting and fishing. More than 40 miles of frontage on the Salmon River. Rugged terrain and beautiful scenery. Adjoins Idaho Primitive Area.

**Sawtooth,** 144,300 acres of the Boise National Forest (headquarters: Boise), 7,900 acres of the Challis National Forest (headquarters: Challis), and 48,742 acres of the Sawtooth National Forest (headquarters: Twin Falls). Scenic terrain featuring the Sawtooth Mountains. Numerous deep gorges and glacial basins, 170 alpine lakes. Fishing good to excellent. Noted for wildlife—deer, elk, mountain goat, bear, mountain lion, small game.

## Montana

**Absaroka,** 64,000 acres of the Gallatin National Forest (headquarters: Bozeman). High mountain area, mainly wooded with lofty peaks. Very good fishing; fair hunting, especially for moose.

**Beartooth,** 175,000 acres of the Custer National Forest (headquarters: Billings), and 55,000 acres of the Gallatin National Forest (headquarters: Bozeman). Rugged high mountain area includes Granite Peak, 12,799 feet (highest in Montana) and Grasshopper Glacier named for millions of grasshoppers entombed in the ice two centuries ago.

**Mission Mountains,** 73,340 acres of the Flathead National Forest (headquarters: Kalispell). High mountainous area of alpine lakes and peaks, containing glaciers and unique glacial evidence. Grizzly bear and mountain goat are found in the area.

**Spanish Peaks,** 49,800 acres of the Gallatin National Forest (headquarters: Bozeman). Wild, moderately rough topography. Outstanding fishing.

## New Mexico

**Gila,** 129,630 acres of the Gila National Forest (headquarters: Silver City). Topography rough to precipitous. Many deep box canyons. Good hunting and trout fishing.

**Black Range,** 169,196 acres of the Gila National Forest (headquarters: Silver City). Rough, forested terrain. Trout fishing and hunting, including the best deer and bear opportunities in New Mexico.

**Blue Range** (also partly in Arizona), 36,598 acres of the Apache National Forest (headquarters: Springerville, Arizona). Traversed by the Mogollon Rim with spruce and fir in the high country above and ponderosa pine in the broken country below. Big game is abundant.

## Oregon

**Mount Jefferson,** 24,514 acres of the Deschutes National Forest (headquarters: Bend), 3,158 acres of the Mount Hood National Forest (headquarters: Portland), and 57,361 acres of the Willamette National Forest (headquarters: Eugene). Snow-capped Mount Jefferson, 10,495 feet, second highest peak in Oregon. Perpetual glaciers and Three Fingered Jack are the main features of this Cascade summit area.

## Utah

**High Uintas,** 164,434 acres of the Ashley National Forest (headquarters: Vernal), and 72,743 acres of the Wasatch National Forest (headquarters: Salt Lake City). The High Uinta Mountains, ranging from 8,000 to 13,449 feet, are the highest in Utah and the only major east-west range in the United States. A wild, picturesque region, rich in scenic, geological and biological interest, noted for fishing in over 250 lakes.

## Washington

**North Cascade,** 434,200 acres of the Mount Baker National Forest (headquarters: Bellingham), and 366,800 acres of the Okanogan National Forest (headquarters: Okanogan). This vast area satisfies the demands of the most strenuous wilderness seeker; he can travel for months without retracing his steps amid some of America's grandest mountain scenery.

## Wyoming

**Cloud Peak,** 137,000 acres of the Bighorn National Forest (headquarters: Sheridan). The glacial sculpture of the Bighorn Range left near-vertical walls of 1,000 to 5,000 feet high. Numerous lakes and remnants of glaciers near Cloud Peak and Blacktooth Mountain.

**Glacier,** 177,000 acres of the Shoshone National Forest (headquarters: Cody). Extremely rugged topography. Includes Fremont Peak, innumerable alpine lakes and some of the largest living glaciers in the United States.

**Popo Agie,** 70,000 acres of the Shoshone National Forest (headquarters: Cody). Extremely rough topography along the Continental Divide. Contains 75 lakes; rich in historical lore.

**Stratified,** 203,930 acres of the Shoshone National Forest (headquarters: Cody). A region of narrow valleys and broad, flat-topped mountains, built up of lava flow. Rich in petrified forest remains. Abundant game.

AREAS UNDER REVIEW
FOR THE
NATIONAL WILDERNESS
PRESERVATION SYSTEM
(presently classified as Primitive Areas)

# Part 4

## Specially Designated Areas for Scenic, Historical, Archeological, Geological and Memorial Protection

### Alabama

**Bee Branch Scenic Area,** 1,112 acres of the Bankhead National Forest (headquarters: Montgomery). The heart of a complete sub-watershed near Haleyville is a deep box canyon with sheer sandstone cliffs. Specimens of mountain hardwoods and hemlocks, and one of the last remnants of virgin cove hardwoods in Alabama, are in this area.

### Alaska

**Tracy Arm-Ford's Terror Scenic Area,** 283,000 acres of the North Tongass National Forest (headquarters: Juneau). Two glacial fjords penetrate into the mountainous mainland of southeastern Alaska. Visitors frequenting the area, principally by boats from Juneau, are awed by icebergs and sheer cliff walls that rise 2,000 feet above dark blue salt water. Two glaciers flow into Tracy Arm, providing continuous icebergs. This glaciated country is a favored haunt of mountain goat.

**Walker Cove-Rudyerd Bay Scenic Area,** 93,540 acres of the South Tongass National Forest (headquarters: Ketchikan). Two salt-water fjords, for which the area is named, wind between sheer in height. Cascading waterfalls form spectacular panoramas. Mountain goats frequently are seen clinging to the nearly vertical walls. Alpine lakes in the mountain valleys offer additional scenery and excellent trout fishing.

**Kasaan Totem Park Archeological Area,** eleven acres of the South Tongass National Forest (headquarters: Ketchikan). Buildings and totems assembled at the edge of Ketchikan are restorations of structures and artifacts made by the Haida Indians during the reign of Chief Son-I-Hat.

### Arizona

**Sycamore Canyon Scenic Area,** 455 acres of the Coronado National Forest (headquarters: Tucson). Located in a rugged mountain canyon east of Pearce in oak-savannah vegetation with elevations ranging from 3,800 to 4,500 feet, the scenic area has been called a "hidden botanical garden." It harbors unusual plant species rarely found in other parts of southern Arizona.

**C. Hart Merriam Scenic Area,** 275 acres of the Coconino National Forest (headquarters: Flagstaff). The area includes the slopes and peak of the San Francisco Peaks and the summit of Arizona's highest mountain, Humphrey's Peak, elevation 12,680 feet, north of Flagstaff. Starkly beautiful massive volcanic rock formations and rare (in Arizona) Arctic-Alpine and Subalpine life zones are highlights. A few bristlecone pines grow in less accessible areas.

### Arkansas

**Blowout Mountain Scenic Area,** 320 acres of the Ouachita National Forest (headquarters: Hot Springs). Mature stand of shortleaf pine with old hardwoods, north of Pencil Bluff.

**Crystal Mountain Scenic Area,** 100 acres of the Ouachita National Forest (headquarters: Hot Springs). Impressiveness is lent by ancient shortleaf pine trees south of Mount Ida, long past their prime of growth. Beneath the upper canopy of limbs, the "understory" has hardwoods including white oak, red oak and gum.

**Dutch Creek Mountain Scenic Area,** 376 acres of the Ouachita National Forest (headquarters: Hot Springs). Excellent old-growth stand of shortleaf pine near Gravelly. Hilly, rocky land affording a picturesque experience for the hiker and lover of wildflowers in season.

**Lake Winona Scenic Area,** 450 acres of the Ouachita National Forest (headquarters: Hot Springs). Extensive stand of near-virgin shortleaf pine. There are also impressive oaks and other hardwoods in the area north of Jessieville.

**Natural Bridge Scenic Area,** 320 acres of the Ozark National Forest (headquarters: Russellville). Typical Ozark Mountain hardwoods north of Fort Douglas, including old-growth white oak, red and black gum, beech, elm, black cherry and hickory.

### California

**Ancient Bristlecone Pine Forest Botanical Area,** 27,160 acres of the Inyo National Forest (headquarters: Bishop). World's oldest living things; some of these trees near Bishop are known to be approximately 4,600 years old. A vegetative association of bristlecone pines from very young to the oldest known.

**Arrowhead Landmark Geological Area,** 40 acres of the San Bernardino National Forest (headquarters: San Bernardino). Peculiar soil formation causing a definite change in vegetation on a large area of steep mountainside overlooking urbanized area north of San Bernardino in southern California. When viewed from urbanized area, a striking resemblance to an Indian arrowhead is seen. Landmark is part of early Indian legend.

**Black Mountain Scenic Area,** 6,691 acres of the San Bernardino National Forest (headquarters: San Bernardino). High country near Idyllwild in southern California notable for huge granite outcrops amid virgin coniferous forest. Many outstanding vista points overlooking the desert to the north and east and the interior valley to the west.

**Burnt Lava Flow Virgin Area,** 8,552 acres of the Modoc National Forest (headquarters: Alturas). A spectacular flow of jumbled black lava surrounding islands of timber on old cinder cones northwest of Alturas. Cones protrude above the flow, with several large craters.

**Calaveras Memorial Scenic Area,** 379 acres of the Stanislaus National Forest (headquarters: Sonora). A magnificent stand of mixed conifer type virgin trees adjacent to the Calaveras South Grove of Big Trees (Sequoia gigantea) State Park near Calaveras. Contains the finest stand of sugar pine in California.

**King Caverns Geological Area,** 379 acres of the Sierra National Forest (headquarters: Fresno). Multicolored limestone formations in underground caverns east of Fresno.

**Packsaddle Cavern Geological Area,** 160 acres of the Sequoia National Forest (headquarters: Porterville). Multicolored limestone formations in underground caverns northeast of Bakersfield.

**Feather Falls Scenic Area,** 8,590 acres of the Plumas National Forest (headquarters: Quincy). Features include granite domes and Feather Falls, on Fall Creek, flowing into the Middle Fork of the Feather River; it is the third highest waterfall in the United States outside of Alaska. (The two taller ones are in Yosemite National Park.) Additional waterfalls are located on the South Branch of the Middle Fork and on the Middle Fork of the Feather River itself. Rock domes and boulders throughout the area provide contrast to the vegetation and water.

### Colorado

**Abyss Lake Scenic Area,** 5,880 acres of the Pike National Forest (headquarters: Colorado Springs). A lake lying at 12,550 foot elevation west of Denver on Mount Evans in a rock-rimmed gorge with a jagged, spectacular background of 14,000-foot mountain. Rugged mountaineering, good trout fishing, opportunity for observing and photographing wildlife is everywhere present. Accessible by hiking from State Highway 5, the highest auto road in the country.

**Lost Creek Scenic Area,** 15,120 acres of the Pike National Forest (headquarters: Colorado Springs). Some of the most spectacular granite formations in Colorado, including domes, half-domes, sheer walls, pinnacles, spires, minarets, and even a natural arch, are to be found in the central portion of the area. Goose Creek nearing its headwaters, ducks in and out of huge granite slides or "sinks" no less than nine times. From the last point of emergence downstream to its source it assumes the name Lost Creek. The area northwest of Colorado Springs not only provides unusual scenery, but spectacular rock climbing, good fishing, and a chance to observe and photograph wildlife, including the Rocky Mountain bighorn sheep.

**Windy Ridge-Bristlecone Pine Scenic Area,** 150 acres of the Pike National Forest (headquarters: Colorado Springs). A small stand of bristlecone pine trees in the Windy Ridge section of Mt. Bross are the attraction near Alma.

## Florida

**Alexander Springs Creek Scenic Area,** 6,600 acres of the Ocala National Forest (headquarters: Tallahassee). The area is bisected by a crystal clear semi-tropical river. Among many tree species are slash pine, sand pine, black pine, loblolly, hardwoods and palms. Abundant biological and zoological species are native to the area north of Eustis.

**Bradwell Bay Scenic Area,** 100 acres of the Apalachicola National Forest (headquarters: Tallahassee). The titi swamp southeast of Tallahassee includes pockets of virgin slash pine ranging up to 36 inches in diameter and 100 feet in height.

**Cathead Pond Historical Area,** one acre of the Ocala National Forest (headquarters: Tallahassee). A small but deep pond alongside the road from Ocala to Fort Gates Landing. Legend has it that during the Civil War a small battle was fought nearby. The winner is supposed to have dumped the loser's cannon and side arms in the pond.

**Davenport Landing Historical Area,** two acres of the Ocala National Forest (headquarters: Tallahassee). Site of a small fort protecting and blocking access up the Oklawaha River—probably built during Civil War or pre-Civil War days. Remnants of gun positions are still evident east of Orange Springs.

**Indian Mounds Archeological Area,** 130 acres of the Ocala National Forest (headquarters: Tallahassee). Three Indian shell mounds in hardwood hammock and swamp northeast of Eustis. Carbon tests show they are from 2,000 to 5,000 years old—probably midden or garbage-type mounds.

**Juniper Springs Creek Scenic Area,** 623 acres of the Ocala National Forest (headquarters: Tallahassee). Lush semi-tropical vegetation framing a clear spring-fed stream running twelve miles from origin to the beautiful St. John River east of Ocala. Multiple species of plant and animal life include herons, alligators, hyacinth and orchids.

**Kimbal Island Scenic Area,** 1,000 acres of the Ocala National Forest (headquarters: Tallahassee). A semi-tropical island exhibiting good examples of Florida hardwood hammock, loblolly pine and hardwood river swamp. A good Indian shell mound, native sour oranges and a few remaining orange and grapefruit trees of late 19th-century groves. The island northeast of Eustis is bound by St. Johns River, Alexander Spring Creek, and river swamp, and is accessible only by boat.

**Lake Charles Scenic Area,** 1,021 acres of the Ocala National Forest (headquarters: Tallahassee). 360-acre lake north of Lynne surrounded by a fringe of swamp, titi, black pine, slash pine, and cypress.

**Leon Sink Geological Area,** 13 acres of the Apalachicola National Forest (headquarters: Tallahassee). An area southeast of Tallahassee with several limestone sinks each significantly different from the other. These include **Dismal**—sheer walls drop to dark forbidding pool below; many good species of hardwood around lip although area is scrub hardwood. **Hammock**—good hardwood timber around sink of clear water and 65-foot-deep caverns. **Natural Bridge**—flowing stream goes underground for about 10-15 yards, pops up again and continues flowing. **Gopher Hole**—shaped like a huge land terrapin den, full of crystal clear water.

**Morrison Hammock Scenic Area,** 300 acres of the Apalachicola National Forest (headquarters: Tallahassee). Nice example of hardwood hammock with specimen trees of spruce pine and loblolly pine throughout. At least one and possibly two boils flowing about a million gallons a day each are attractions southeast of Tallahassee.

**Rocky Bluff Scenic Area,** 222 acres of the Apalachicola National Forest (headquarters: Tallahassee). Multiple botanical specimens rich in dogwood, redbud, located on bluff overlooking the Ochlockonee River southeast of Tallahassee.

## Georgia

**Anna Ruby Falls Scenic Area,** 1,600 acres of the Chattahoochee National Forest (headquarters: Gainesville). Two waterfalls from York and Curtiss Creeks intersect at the base of each falls to form Smith Creek north of Robertstown. Free water falls about 50 and 155 feet, respectively, from these falls, yielding nearly four miles of fast flowing mountain streams. Rhododendron and other flowering trees and shrubs are prevalent.

*Twist Falls in Snoqualmie National Forest, Washington.*

**Blood Mountain Archeological Area,** 28 acres of the Chattahoochee National Forest (headquarters: Gainesville). Georgia's third highest mountain. The noted battle between the Creek and Cherokee Indians took place here north of Turner's Corner before 1800. The streams below ran red with blood. The home of Nunneli or spirit people, according to Cherokee myth. The area is covered with purple and white rhododendron, azalea, mountain laurel; colt's foot is a feature in May.

**Coleman River Scenic Area,** 330 acres of the Chattahoochee National Forest (headquarters: Gainesville). On the west side of Coleman River with difficult accessibility by trail. This mountain area south of Tate City of mostly uncut virgin watershed land drops steeply from ridge top to riverbed. Portions were burned in 1949. The river-bottom presents scenic beauty of the first order, swift water over large boulders and rich shrubberies of laurel, rhododendron, azalea, leucothoe, dogwood and ferns. Nearby on Tallulah River is a developed camping area for those who want to stay and explore.

**Cooper Creek Scenic Area,** 1,240 acres of the Chattahoochee National Forest (headquarters: Gainesville). Beautiful Cooper Creek and tributaries south of Blairsville are sparkling and full of trout. There are some notable white pines, white oaks and hemlocks.

**DeSoto Falls Scenic Area,** 650 acres of the Chattahoochee National Forest (headquarters: Gainesville). Area contains five scenic waterfalls and five miles of mountain streams north of Turner's Corner. Flowering trees and shrubs including rhododendron, laurel, azalea, dogwood, sourwood and other species are abundant.

**High Shoals Creek Falls Scenic Area,** 170 acres of the Chattahoochee National Forest (headquarters: Gainesville). Here a succession of five waterfalls is the feature, with luxuriant banks of rhododendron and laurel bordering the sparkling stream. An old road south of Hiawassee climbing the mountainside affords a convenient access from which the pedestrian can strike off at several levels and descend to the respective waterfalls. Mountain hardwood trees in variety of sizes and species adorn the gorge.

**Keown Falls Scenic Area,** 231 acres of the Chattahoochee National Forest (headquarters: Gainesville). A pair of picturesque falls, the larger of which gives the area its name. The trees have aspects of virgin pristine watershed. The area south of Villanow abounds in squirrel, deer, turkey, grouse and other forest animals.

**Raven Cliff Scenic Area,** 1,589 acres of the Chattahoochee National Forest (headquarters: Gainesville). The unique feature of cascading Dodd Creek, west of Robertstown, is Raven Cliff Falls, which splits a 150-foot solid rock face before cascading into a deep pool.

**Scull Shoals Historical Area,** 34 acres of the Oconee National Forest (headquarters: Gainesville). The vegetation is piedmont bottom land, hardwood type, subject to occasional overflow. Remnants of the abandoned town of Scull Shoals consisting of building foundations, chimneys and bridges are the points of interest. This site, north of Greensboro, settled in 1784, figured in numerous massacres by the Indians. Georgia's first paper mill, possibly the South's, was built here during the War of 1812; the area is also the site of Georgia's first cotton gin and cotton factory in 1834.

**Scull Shoals Indian Mound Archeological Area,** 66 acres of the Oconee National Forest (headquarters: Gainesville). The vegetation is piedmont bottom land, hardwood type, subject to occasional overflow from the Oconee River. Significant archeologically, remains of a two mound prehistoric Indian Village, a temple mound and the intervening area of occupation once containing probably the "square ground" (for Indian ball games), this gleaned from Bartram's travels of the late 1700's. Actually the mounds at Scull Shoals constitute one of the best extant examples of a Creek Indian Village as graphically described by Bartram.

**Sosebee Cove Scenic Area,** 175 acres of the Chattahoochee National Forest (headquarters: Gainesville). This area south of Blairsville is rich in botanical lore. The feature is the 25-acre stand of virgin yellow poplar—an impressive experience. Other trees in large size run the gamut of Appalachian hardwoods and pines. The forest floor harbors 30 species of wild flowers; some are rare ones such as Dutchman's-breeches and snowy orchids.

**Track Rock Gap Historical Site,** 52 acres of the Chattahoochee National Forest (headquarters: Gainesville). An area south of Jacksonville with preserved petroglyphs of ancient Indian origin from which the Gap gets its name. These carvings resemble animal and bird tracks, also crosses, circles and human footprints. Protective grilles have been installed over the carvings and an appropriate parking area is provided beside the highway. The history is given on a wooden plaque and a roadside historic marker.

## Idaho

**Hells Canyon-Seven Devils Scenic Area** (also partly in Oregon), 94,810 acres of the Payette and Nezperce National Forests (headquarters: McCall and Grangeville). The deepest gorge in North America, "Hells Canyon," and seven volcanic peaks, "Seven Devils," aptly describe the principal features of this spectacular area between Homedale and Lewiston. Elevation changes of 5,500 feet in four miles reveal rugged topography with extremely steep slopes. The area abounds in magnificent scenery, geologic features, artifacts and petroglyphs, big and small game and a great variety of fishing.

**Sacajawea Historical Area** (also partly in Montana), 58 acres of the Salmon National Forest (headquarters: Salmon). The area lies on both sides of Lemhi Pass on the Montana-Idaho boundary and Continental Divide south of Salmon. In 1805, Sacajawea guided the Lewis and Clark party over this pass. This event inspired Lewis to record his personal satisfaction at having reached the westward flowing waters. Designated as a National Historic Site.

## Illinois

**La Rue Scenic Area,** 983 acres of the Shawnee National Forest (headquarters: Harrisburg). Scenic combination of hills and river bottom near Aldredge. High sandstone bluffs rising precipitously present a striking appearance. The river bottom is a combination of swamp, shallow waters, and land supporting excellent stands of hardwoods with a variety of animal life. Of special interest is a species of blind fish, an egret rookery, the cliff rat, and waterfowl during the migratory periods.

## Kentucky

**Yahoo Falls Scenic Area,** 230 acres of the Daniel Boone National Forest (headquarters: Winchester). A waterfall south of Somerset where Yahoo Creek breaks over a cliff. Fall is about 80 feet high and varies seasonally. In the spring there is a rushing volume; this changes to a ribbon-type fall in summer and in the winter an ice cone builds up at the base of the falls, sometimes to a height of 30 to 50 feet. Surrounding area has beautiful gray, orange and red sandstone cliffs. Hemlock, white oak and poplar grow below the cliffs.

**Natural Arch Scenic Area,** 945 acres of the Daniel Boone National Forest (headquarters: Winchester). Large sandstone arch about 75 feet high and 150 feet long, formed by wind and water erosion. Exposed cliff lines give the arch a distinctive canyon setting. Cove hardwoods and hemlock grow in the hollows grading into pine on the ridgetops south of Somerset.

## Louisiana

**Castor Creek Scenic Area,** 90 acres of the Kisatchie National Forest (headquarters: Alexandria). Centered at the junction of two creeks southwest of Alexandria, the area includes a stand of unusually large loblolly pine, gum, ash, beech, magnolia and cypress.

**Kisatchie Hills Scenic Area,** 420 acres of the Kisatchie National Forest (headquarters: Alexandria) "Near-natural" aptly describes this area north of Gorum, cut over very long ago, again attaining virginal aspect. The vegetation is longleaf pine at its best. The topography (elevation over 300 feet) characterized by rocky, eroded hills, is unique in Louisiana.

**Longleaf Scenic Area,** 28 acres of the Kisatchie National Forest (headquarters: Alexandria). Pure stands of old-growth longleaf pine about 100 years old which were left when the country east of Rosepine was logged in the early 1930's.

## Michigan

**Loda Lake Scenic Area,** 58 acres of the Manistee National Forest (headquarters: Cadillac). The great attraction of this area north of

Grand Rapids is the profusion of many species of wildflowers in a forest environment. The forest together with the blooming plants surrounding a small undeveloped lake, makes an excellent scenic combination.

**Round Island Scenic Area,** 352 acres of the Hiawatha National Forest (headquarters: Escanaba). Round Island is located between historic Mackinac and Bois Blanc Islands, in the Straits of Mackinac between Lake Michigan and Lake Huron; a historic crossroads of early fur trade. Located on it is an abandoned lighthouse built in 1873. One of the few remaining undeveloped large islands in the Great Lakes. Visitors crossing the Mackinac Straits Bridge can enjoy a charming view of its natural beauty.

**The Lumberman's Monument Historical Site,** three acres of the Huron National Forest (headquarters: Cadillac). A three-figure bronze memorial depicting a timber cruiser, tree faller and river driver commemorating the loggers who cut the virgin timber in Michigan in the latter part of the 19th century. It is located northwest of East Tawas on a scenic site overlooking the Au Sable River which was the scene of many a log drive.

## Mississippi

**Bienville Pines Scenic Area,** 189 acres of the Bienville National Forest (headquarters: Jackson). The largest known stand of pine left uncut in the state is found south of the town of Forest. It includes large specimens of loblolly and shortleaf pine up to 200 years old.

**Owl Creek Mounds Archeological Area,** 30 acres of the Tombigbee National Forest (headquarters: Jackson). Five Indian mounds arranged around a plaza offer evidence of aboriginal people of the period 400 to 800 A.D.

*Caribou Lake in Caribou Wilderness Area, Lassen National Forest.*

SPECIALLY DESIGNATED AREAS
FOR SCENIC, HISTORICAL,
ARCHAEOLOGICAL, GEOLOGICAL
AND MEMORIAL PROTECTION

*Natural arch weathered from conglomerate on Specimen Ridge, Gallatin National Forest.*

## Missouri

**Current and Eleven Point Rivers Scenic Area**, 20,239 acres of the Mark Twain National Forest (headquarters: Springfield). The area along these free-flowing rivers is rough, forested, scenic Ozark country. Hills rise above the streams with many impressive cliffs and ravines. The streams support a good population of fish. Float fishing in the traditional "Johnboats" is a popular recreational activity.

## Montana

**Madison River Canyon Earthquake Geological Area**, 36,415 acres of Gallatin National Forest (headquarters: Bozeman). Established to protect and explain the spectacular evidence of the August 17, 1959, earthquake northwest of West Yellowstone. Features include a huge slide which blocked off the Madison River, creating a five-mile-long lake, fault scarps, blow holes, and destruction of highways and buildings.

**Northwest Peaks Scenic Area**, 6,922 acres of the Kootenai National Forest (headquarters: Libby), and the Kaniksu National Forest (headquarters: Sandpoint, Idaho). Three rugged peaks east of Addie rise above timberline, surrounded by seven glacial lakes.

**Ross Creek Scenic Area**, 100 acres of the Kootenai National Forest (headquarters: Libby). Northeast of Clark Fork, this is one of few remaining pure stands of virgin, old-growth cedar. Trees are up to twelve feet in diameter at breast height. The canopy is dense with little or no undergrowth on the forest floor.

**Sacajawea Historical Area** (also partly in Idaho), 83 acres of the Beaverhead National Forest (headquarters: Dillon). The area lies on both sides of Lemhi Pass on the Montana-Idaho boundary and Continental Divide south of Salmon. In 1805 Sacajawea guided the Lewis and Clark party over this pass. This event inspired Lewis to record his personal satisfaction at having reached the westward flowing waters. Designated as a National Historical Site.

**Ten Lakes Scenic Area**, 6,541 acres of the Kootenai National Forest (headquarters: Libby). A high subalpine region outside Eureka embraces scenic peaks, glacial lakes and mountain meadows.

## Nevada

**Ruby Mountain Scenic Area**, 38,610 acres of the Humboldt National Forest (headquarters: Elko). Lamoille Canyon, the most prominent feature of this narrow range (about 100 miles long and only eight to nine miles wide) near Lamoille, was carved by an immense glacier with sheer walls rising 2,000 feet. Starting at Lamoille Lake, at the base of an 11,000 foot peak, it cuts a semi-circular course through the west side of the Ruby Mountains. Trails lead from the road end at the head of the canyon to Liberty Lake and the top of the range. The rugged, intensely glaciated crest of the Rubies is dominated by ten peaks over 10,000 feet, with two dozen alpine lakes nestled among its cirques.

**Wheeler Peak Scenic Area**, 28,000 acres of the Humboldt National Forest (headquarters: Elko). Wheeler Peak, east of Ely, is 13,063 feet in elevation, the highest point wholly within the State of Nevada. The area includes a rock glacier and perennial snow field on the slope of Wheeler Peak; the largest mountain mahogany tree on record; gnarled bristlecone pine trees, thousands of years old; small alpine lakes; flora representing four life zones; a large deer herd, and magnificent desert views.

## New Hampshire

**Gibbs Brook Scenic Area**, 900 acres of the White Mountain National Forest (headquarters: Laconia). Highlights include stands of virgin spruce, rugged mountain topography, and the historic Crawford Path of 1819. A section of the Appalachian Trail traverses the upper reaches of the area south of Bretton Woods.

**Greeley Ponds Scenic Area**, 810 acres of the White Mountain National Forest (headquarters: Laconia). Virgin red spruce and balsam fir with two picturesque ponds are isolated by rugged cliffs and rock-slide-scarred mountain slopes north of Waterville.

**Lafayette Brook Scenic Area**, 900 acres of the White Mountain National Forest (headquarters: Laconia). Towering Mount Lafayette, Eagle Cliff and Eagle Lakes are impressive. Several landslides scar the upper reaches of Lafayette Brook. The vegetative cover ranges from old-growth spruce to hardwood in the lower reaches. Alpine grasses and flowering plants above 4,500 foot elevation along the Appalachian Trail south of Franconia.

**Nancy Brook Scenic Area,** 460 acres of the White Mountain National Forest (headquarters: Laconia). Nancy Brook, west of Notchland, cascades in 200-foot leaps from glacier-formed Nancy Pond past virgin red spruce clinging to narrow valley walls. It was named for a young woman who drowned in the stream in 1780.

**Pinkham Notch Scenic Area,** 5,600 acres of the White Mountain National Forest (headquarters: Laconia). Eastern slopes of Mount Washington, the highest mountain in Northeast United States with great ravines cut into its sides. Skiing at Tuckerman Ravine until mid-June; summer hiking at Huntington Ravine. Alpine Gardens noted for rare arctic flora attracts many botanists. Glen Ellis Falls, 64 feet high—spectacular and widely known in the White Mountains.

**Rocky Gorge Scenic Area,** 70 acres of the White Mountain National Forest (headquarters: Laconia). Rocky Gorge is formed where the Swift River plunges over broken ledges into a gorge worn through solid rock to a depth of 20 feet. Falls Pond is a six-acre natural impoundment of glacial origin. Picnic facilities developed. The scenic Kancamagus Highway passes through the eastern edge of the area west of Conway.

**Sawyer Pond Scenic Area,** 1,130 acres of the White Mountain National Forest (headquarters: Laconia). Two ponds of glacial origin are overshadowed by the towering rugged cliff faces of Mount Tremont and Owls Cliff. Sawyer Pond, 46 acres in size, has an average depth of 44 feet. Little Sawyer Pond, six acres in size, averages 14 feet in depth. Brook-trout fishing is good in both ponds west of Bartlett.

**Snyder Brook Scenic Area,** 36 acres of the White Mountain National Forest (headquarters: Laconia). Gordon Falls, Salroc Falls and Tama Falls consist of a series of remarkable cascades. In combination with the old-growth timber stands, they provide an extremely pleasing attraction south of Randolph.

# North Carolina

**Craggy Mountain Scenic Area,** 950 acres of the Pisgah National Forest (headquarters: Asheville). The heart of the area is a gigantic original stand of Canadian hemlock, but a heterogeneity of mountain hardwoods exists in this large elevated valley immediately under the Blue Ridge Parkway near Craggy Gardens. In the midst of the hemlock is beautiful Waterfall Creek Falls, gained by trail. Elevations are in the 4,000's.

**Ellicott Rock Scenic Area,** 3,584 acres shared among the Nantahala National Forest (headquarters: Asheville), Sumter National Forest (headquarters: Columbia, South Carolina), and Chattahoochee National Forest (headquarters: Gainesville, Georgia). The focal point of the area is the "Corner Rock," where South Carolina, North Carolina and Georgia meet, named for the early surveyor John Ellicott (also prominent for his survey work in the design of Washington, D. C.). With stands of virgin trees, isolated cascades and waterfalls, the area gives the impression of a mountain wilderness as it must have been in pre-colonial days. It embraces the site of a Cherokee Indian village and a Creek trading trail.

**John's Rock Scenic Area,** 435 acres of the Pisgah National Forest (headquarters: Asheville). A scenic granite monolith with 200-foot cliffs glistens in the sunlight above the Davidson River west of Brevard.

**Joyce Kilmer Memorial Forest,** 3,840 acres of the Nantahala National Forest (headquarters: Asheville). At the head of Lake Santeetlah, north of Robbinsville, this mountain cove of virgin hardwood forest draws lovers of the unmodified wilderness. In temperate zone rain forest are yellow poplars 84 feet in diameter and hemlocks 76 inches in diameter. Lesser giants number into the hundreds. Development has provided access roads and an extensive trail system to the Joyce Kilmer Memorial Plaque, 1½ miles up the cove.

**Looking Glass Rock Scenic Area,** 1,600 acres of the Pisgah National Forest (headquarters: Asheville). The much photographed towering monolith is found on the same scenic drive as John's Rock. It is named for its glistening sides, the result of water seepage from bordering forest vegetation.

**Whitewater River Falls Scenic Area,** 266 acres of the Nantahala National Forest (headquarters: Asheville). Whitewater River Falls, south of Oakland, is one of the most spectacular in the Eastern United States. The total drop is reported to be 411 feet and occurs within a distance of 500 feet in several cascades.

**Glenn Falls Scenic Area,** 120 acres of the Nantahala National Forest (headquarters: Asheville). Spectacular waterfalls splash over plate rock formations west of Highlands.

# Oregon

**Hells Canyon-Seven Devils Scenic Area,** 32,500 acres of the Wallowa-Whitman National Forests (headquarters: Baker). The scenic canyon of Snake River between Homedale and Lewiston has rough precipitous, rock walls; outstanding views from high above river; elevations vary from 1,335 feet on the Snake to 9,389 feet in Seven Devils Mountains; upper Seven Devils marked with frequent alpine lakes. (See further description in Idaho portion of area.)

**Lamb Butte Scenic Area,** 390 acres of the Willamette National Forest (headquarters: Eugene). This peninsula of the High Cascades is surrounded by the older Western Cascades. It includes a glacial cirque with small circular ponds of various depths and temperatures known as the Potholes and outstanding views of the Three Sisters Mountains east of Eugene.

**Lava Cast Geological Area,** 5,630 acres of the Deschutes National Forest (headquarters: Bend). Tree molds on "lava casts," "lava falls," crevices and fissures are found south of Bend. The area is surrounded by volcanic cinder cones.

**Lavacicle Cave Geological Area,** 40 acres of the Deschutes National Forest (headquarters: Bend). A myriad of lava stalactites and stalagmites were formed by the cave being sealed and remaining intensely hot. The lava drippings resulted in these spectacular formations south of Bend.

**Lowder Mountain Geological Area,** 140 acres of the Willamette National Forest (headquarters: Eugene). An extensive open summit east of Eugene is a remnant of the original Pliocene vulcanism, with relict islands of xeric flora, characterized by aridity, or moisture deficiency.

**Quaking Aspen Swamp Botanical Area,** 240 acres of the Willamette National Forest (headquarters: Eugene). A glacial cirque contains a prime example of a mountain sphagnum bog with typical bog plants east of Eugene.

**Rebel Rock Geological Area,** 700 acres of the Willamette National Forest (headquarters: Eugene). Rugged rock outcroppings east of Eugene are an example of Pliocene vulcanism. It includes relict islands of xeric flora.

**Umpqua Dunes Scenic Area,** 2,760 acres of the Siuslaw National Forest (headquarters: Corvallis). Outstanding dune formations on the Pacific Coast extend inland about two miles, and the dunes rise to a height of about 300 feet. Islands of ancient stabilized dunes exist within the area near Lakeside.

**Yankee Mountain Scenic Area,** 490 acres of the Willamette National Forest (headquarters: Eugene). Characteristic of the older Western Cascades, there are views into the South Fork of the McKenzie River drainage from forest openings. The area east of Eugene offers impressive examples of dissection of the older Cascades into deep canyons and residual mountains.

**Big Craggies Botanical Area,** 3,800 acres of the Siskiyou National Forest (headquarters: Grants Pass). Rare flora, primarily **Kalmiopsis leachiana** and Brewer spruce, are the unique features in this section of the mountains south of Medford.

**Cape Perpetua Scenic Area,** 988 acres of the Siuslaw National Forest (headquarters: Corvallis). Cape Perpetua, south of Waldport, rises abruptly from the sea to 800 feet, then climbs gradually to more than

1,400 feet. It is one of the finest features along the Oregon Coast, with vestiges of an ancient settlement preserved in an archeological area, and two geological areas. The Forest Service operates a visitor information center.

**Cascade Head Scenic Area,** 250 acres of the Siuslaw National Forest (headquarters: Corvallis). Cascade Head rises sharply from the ocean in precipitous cliffs, 100 to 300 feet high west of Neskowin. The Head itself climbs eastward to an elevation of 1,700 feet, three miles inland, with a great variety of shrubs and flowers. Cross-country travel is dangerous in the area, especially above the ocean shore.

**Little Crater Lake Geological Area,** five acres of the Mount Hood National Forest (headquarters: Portland). This small lake of unknown origin east of Portland has striking setting and characteristics. The water is deep blue in color and extremely clear.

**Lava Butte Geological Area,** 3,983 acres of the Deschutes National Forest (headquarters: Bend). Some of the most spectacular volcanic formations in America are located in central Oregon south of Bend. Lava Butte, a cinder cone, rises 500 feet above the adjacent forest-covered country, overlooking areas of dramatic volcanism and scenic beauty.

**Marion Lake Scenic Area,** 1,596 acres of the Willamette National Forest (headquarters: Eugene). Mountain lakes, Marion and Ann, as well as spectacular Marion Falls, are accessible by foot trails in the area south of Detroit.

# Pennsylvania

**Hearts Content Scenic Area,** 275 acres of the Allegheny National Forest (headquarters: Warren). This is a 120-acre primeval forest of towering white pine and hardwoods. Parts of the land were presented to the Government by a lumber company and women's clubs.

**Tionesta Scenic Area,** 1,967 acres of the Allegheny National Forest (headquarters: Warren). Located about 15 miles east of Hearts Content, Tionesta embraces magnificent virgin hardwoods and Eastern hemlock, a vestige of typical original growth of the Allegheny Plateau.

# South Carolina

**Broad River Scenic Area,** 210 acres of the Sumter National Forest (headquarters: Columbia). A large hardwood stand northeast of Maykinton on the west bank of the Broad River has specimen trees of oak, hickory and gum with impressive heights and form.

**Guilliard Lake Scenic Area,** 925 acres of the Francis Marion National Forest (headquarters: Columbia). The small finger-shaped lake is central feature, bordered by old-growth bottomland-hardwood trees east of Jamestown. Included are red gum, cow oak, overcup oak, water oak, holly, sycamore and willow.

**Little Wambaw Swamp,** 1,025 acres of the Francis Marion National Forest (headquarters: Columbia). The typical "creek swamp" contains mixture of swamp and tupelo gum along with bald cypress, a few red maples and other hardwoods. Sweet bay, Southern bayberry and leucothoe are common. The area south of McClellanville affords a feeling of expansive wilderness in a pristine forest setting. Undergrowth is light because of frequent flooding.

**Long Cane Scenic Area,** 650 acres of the Sumter National Forest (headquarters: Columbia). Beautiful Long Cane Creek, east of Abbeville, is banked with cane brakes known to reach a height of 20-30 feet and two-three inches in diameter. Mixed pine hardwood trees include black and red gum, water oak, cottonwood, sycamore, hackberry, red maple and loblolly pine.

# Tennessee

**Falls Branch Scenic Area,** 178 acres of the Cherokee National Forest (headquarters: Cleveland). Both the show of virgin timber and the 70-foot waterfalls are spectacular. The outstanding species is virgin black cherry. A jungle of huge rhododendron hems in the area east of Tellico Plains. There is a threshold parking and picnic area at the Forest road leading to a narrow trail down to the falls. Poplars, hemlocks and oaks predominate among the trees.

**Rock Creek Scenic Area,** 220 acres of the Cherokee National Forest (headquarters: Cleveland). A section of a clear mountain stream east of Erwin flows through a steep rugged gorge, broken by eleven waterfalls along its course.

**Unaka Mountain Scenic Area,** 1,100 acres of the Cherokee National Forest (headquarters: Cleveland). This is essentially a virgin remnant of the impressive red spruce-Fraser fir forest that formerly clothed the whole top of mile-high Unaka Mountain. The area east of Erwin also has rhododendron, white and pink flame azaleas, mountain laurel and vacciniums. Elevations range from 3,100 to 4,800 feet.

**Watagua Scenic Area,** 1,100 acres of the Cherokee National Forest (headquarters: Cleveland). Elevations east of Hampton range from 1,980 on the highway to the top of Pond Mountain—elevation 4,329. The upper area is extremely rugged with rock outcrops on the hillsides.

# Texas

**Big Thicket Scenic Area,** 1,130 acres of the Sam Houston National Forest (headquarters: Lufkin). This area northwest of Shepherd is representative of the original Big Thicket, characterized by American beech and other hardwoods and the ubiquitous, thickety yaupon (**Ilex vomitoria**) a red-berried shrub holly. Thicket flora is impressively abundant due to the many spring fed bogs, the lush biotic community typified by viburnum and various ferns.

**East Hamilton Scenic Area,** 105 acres of the Sabine National Forest (headquarters: Lufkin). Between the creek and Sabine River east of Patroon rears a high, bluffy ridge, part of the "river-swamp fringe." The area includes large specimens (six to eight feet in diameter) of bald cypress.

**Yellowpine Scenic Area,** seven acres of the Sabine National Forest (headquarters: Lufkin). The area east of Hemphill consists of virgin shortleaf pine, a small but magnificent sample.

# Utah

**Grove of the Aspen Giants Scenic Area,** ten acres of the Manti-La Sal National Forest (headquarters: Price). Located within this small tract east of Mayfield is a grove of about 20 giant living aspen trees up to 36 inches in diameter. Two older trees, now dead, reached a diameter of over 40 inches. These giant aspen are some of the largest in the world and are exceptionally rare.

**Mount Timpanogos Scenic Area,** 10,750 acres of the Uinta National Forest (headquarters: Provo). This highly scenic area, readily accessible from the principal cities of Utah and Salt Lake valleys, is dominated by Mount Timpanogos, called "Sleeping Lady" in Indian legend, towering to 11,750 feet. Other features include Timpanogos ice field or glacieret, beautiful falls and cascades, many species of big and small game and a well-known Indian trail.

**Sheep Creek Canyon Geological Area,** 3,600 acres of the Ashley National Forest (headquarters: Vernal). An immense earth fracture, the Uinta Crest fault, exposes geologic formations and fossil remains providing a remarkably clear picture of life endless ages in the past. Sheep Creek Canyon, west of Dutch John and south of Manila in Flaming Gorge National Recreation Area, passes through formations laid down millions of years before the coming of man. Other attractions are Sheep Creek Cave, superlative scenery and outstanding fishing and hunting.

*Custer National Forest, South Dakota: Geological formation known as the Honey Combs.*

# Virginia

**Mountain Lake Scenic Area,** 1,543 acres of the Jefferson National Forest (headquarters: Roanoke). Examples of virgin red spruce, hemlock, rhododendron, and rare herb species are among 900 kinds of flowering plants that have been inventoried south of Kare. Elevation 2,040-4,050 feet, with sheer cliffs.

# Washington

**Roosevelt Grove of Ancient Cedars Scenic Area,** 420 acres of the Kaniksu National Forest (headquarters: Sandpoint, Idaho). Two groves of Western red cedar include huge trees up to twelve feet in diameter and 150 feet tall, with average age of 800 years. Granite Creek with cataracts and falls passes through the area north of Nordman.

# West Virginia

**Cranberry Glades Botanical Area,** 750 acres of the Monongahela National Forest (headquarters: Elkins). The appearance of this biologically unique area of open bogs, dense shrubs and northern hardwoods is likened to Arctic tundra. The Glades, east of Richwood, contain the southernmost known specimens of several plants and at least five birds.

**Falls of Hills Creek Scenic Area,** 114 acres of the Monongahela National Forest (headquarters: Elkins). A series of waterfalls as high as 65 feet fall between steep slopes clothed with huge hemlock and northern hardwoods east of Richwood.

**Gaudineer Scenic Area,** 140 acres of the Monongahela National Forest (headquarters: Elkins). Virgin spruce and northern hardwoods comprise an impressive stand of trees north of Durbin.

# Wyoming

**Gros Ventre Slide Geological Area,** 1,458 acres of the Teton National Forest (headquarters: Jackson). A massive land slide slipped on June 23, 1925, displacing some 50 million cubic yards of earth and rock. This raw wound on Sheep Mountain north of Jackson remains a grim reminder of nature's awesome power.

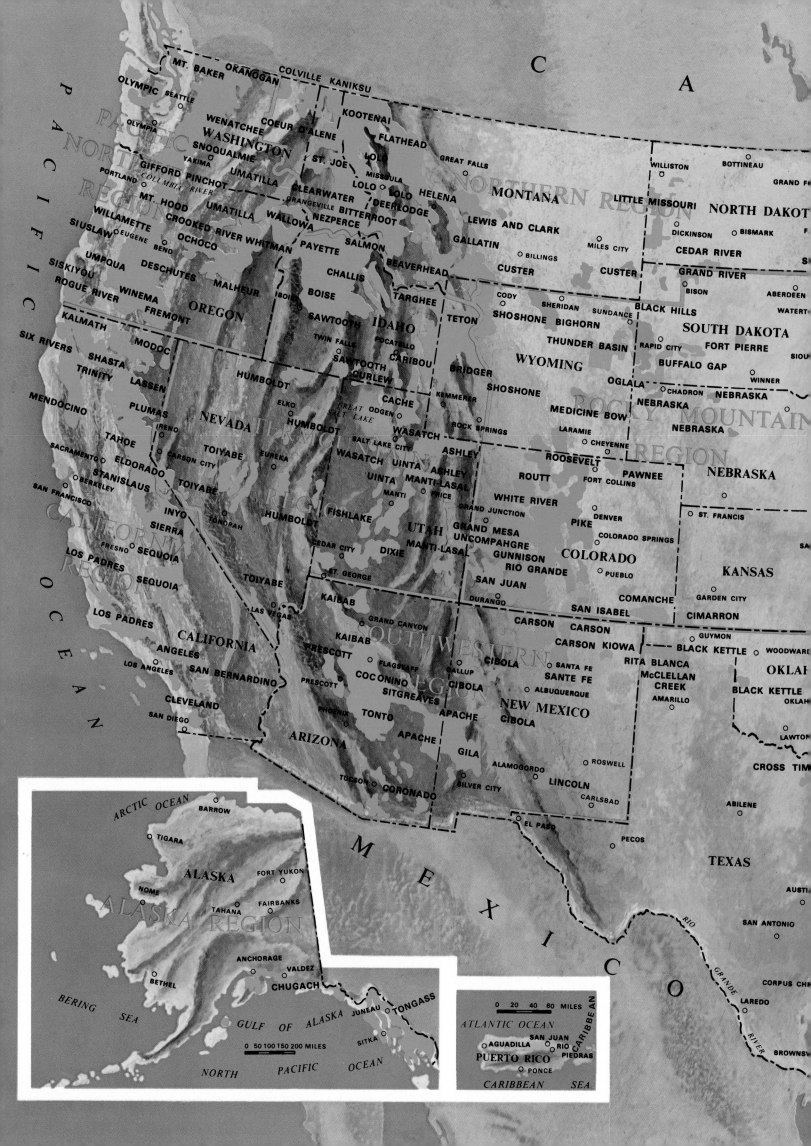

# NATIONAL FORESTS

SCALE 1:10,000,000

100  0  100  200  300  400  500  MILES

**LEGEND**

NATIONAL FORESTS

NATIONAL GRASSLANDS

REGIONAL BOUNDARIES

*Humboldt National Forest, Nevada: Jarbidge Creek, one of the area's many popular fishing streams.*